The POCKET

ORLANDO

Orlando: Regions and Best places to see

★ Best places to see 26–47

■ Featured sight

Orlando 50–73

Around Orlando 74–100

Walt Disney World® Resort
101–129

Original text by Emma Stanford

Updated by Donna Dailey

© Automobile Association Developments Limited 2008. First published 2008

ISBN: 978-0-7495-5763-8

Published by AA Publishing, a trading name of Automobile Association Developments Limited, whose registered office is Fanum House, Basing View, Basingstoke, Hampshire RG21 4EA. Registered number 1878835.

Colour separation: Keenes, Andover
Printed and bound in Italy by Printer Trento S.r.l.

Front cover images: (t) AA/T Harris; (b) AA/P Bennett
Back cover image: AA/P Bennett

A03604
Maps in this title produced from
Map data © Global Mapping 2007
Transport map © Communicarta Ltd, UK

About this book

Symbols are used to denote the following categories:

✚ map reference

✉ address or location

☎ telephone number

🕐 opening times

✋ admission charge

🍴 restaurant or café on premises
or nearby

Ⓜ nearest underground train station

🚌 nearest bus/tram route

🚉 nearest overground train station

⛴ nearest ferry stop

✈ nearest airport

❓ other practical information

ℹ tourist information office

➤ indicates the page where you will
find a fuller description

This book is divided into four sections.

Planning pages 12–25
Before you go; Getting there; Getting
around; Being there

Best places to see pages 26–47
The unmissable highlights of any visit
to Orlando

Exploring pages 48–129
The best places to visit in Orlando,
organized by area

Maps pages 133–144
All map references are to the atlas
section. For example, Discovery Cove
has the reference ✚ 136 C4 –
indicating the page number and grid
square in which it can be found

Contents

Planning

Before you go

WHEN TO GO

JAN	FEB	MAR	APR	MAY	JUN	JUL	AUG	SEP	OCT	NOV	DEC
22°C	23°C	25°C	27°C	27°C	30°C	32°C	32°C	30°C	28°C	25°C	22°C
72°F	73°F	77°F	81°F	81°F	86°F	90°F	90°F	86°F	82°F	77°F	72°F

High season Low season

The warmest months in Orlando are July–August with temperatures reaching highs of 92°F (33°C) and lows of 73°F (23°C). Even in the coolest month of January temperatures can still reach 72°F (22°C) but they can also dip to as low as 49°F (9°C).

Summer storms in July normally see this month being the wettest as well as the hottest with up to 7.8in (20cm) of rain falling in contrast to only 1.8in (5cm) from November to December. In these sticky summer months the mornings are often fine and dry, with thunderstorms more common in the afternoon – in most cases you can queue under cover but it is wise to pack waterproofs or buy a waterproof poncho from one of the many merchandise carts at the parks.

The chart figures above are the average daily maximum for each month.

WHAT YOU NEED

● Required
○ Suggested
▲ Not required

Some countries require a passport to remain valid for a minimum period (usually at least six months) beyond the date of entry.

	UK	Germany	USA	Netherlands	Spain
Passport/ National Identity Card	●	●	▲	●	●
Visa (Waiver form to be completed)	▲	▲	▲	▲	▲
Onward or Return Ticket	●	●	▲	●	●
Health Inoculations (tetanus)	○	○	○	○	○
Health Documentation (► 15, Health insurance)	▲	▲	▲	▲	▲
Travel Insurance	●	●	●	●	●
Driving Licence (national or International Driving Permit)	●	●	●	●	●
Car Insurance Certificate	○	○	●	○	○
Car Registration Document	●	●	●	●	●

WEBSITES

Further details on attractions, dining, shopping, nightlife and recreation are available from:

www.orlandoinfo.com/uk
www.floridakiss.com
www.floridastateparks.org
www.floridatraveluse.com

TOURIST OFFICES AT HOME

In the UK

Orlando/Kissimmee–St. Cloud Tourism Bureau, Inc. Visitor information and a free Orlando/Kissimmee pack of visitor guides to both areas and local map ☎ 020 7233 2305 or 0800 092 2352 (brochure line)

Visit Florida

For an *Official Florida Holiday Guide* ☎ 01737 644882 in the UK. Visit Florida also provide a free phone tourist assistance hotline in Florida ☎ 1-800 656 8777 or 888/735-2872. Further information from www.visitflorida.com

HEALTH INSURANCE

Medical insurance cover of at least $1,000,000 unlimited cover is strongly recommended, as medical bills can be astronomical and treatment may be withheld if you have no evidence of means to pay. Your medical insurance cover should include dental treatment, which is readily available, but expensive. Have a check up before you go. Dental referral telephone numbers are in the Yellow Pages telephone directory or ask at the desk of your hotel.

TIME DIFFERENCES

| GMT 12 noon | Orlando 7AM | Germany 1PM | USA (NY) 7AM | Netherlands 1PM | Spain 1PM |

Orlando local time is Eastern Standard Time (the same as New York) which is five hours behind Greenwich Mean Time (GMT–5). Daylight saving applies, with clocks one hour ahead between March and October.

NATIONAL HOLIDAYS

Jan 1 *New Year's Day*
Jan (third Mon) *Martin Luther King Day*
Feb (third Mon) *Presidents' Day*
Mar/Apr *Good Friday*

May (last Mon) *Memorial Day*
Jul 4 *Independence Day*
Sep (first Mon) *Labor Day*
Oct (second Mon) *Columbus Day*
Nov 11 *Veterans' Day*

Nov (fourth Thu) *Thanksgiving*
Dec 25 *Christmas Day*
Boxing Day is not a public holiday in the US. Some shops open on National Holidays.

WHAT'S ON WHEN

January *Capital One Bowl:* Nationally televised college football game on New Year's Day.
February *Festival of Rhythm & Blues:* Celebrates Black History Month at Kissimmee Lakefront Park.
Silver Spurs Rodeo: Major event on the Professional Rodeo Cowboys Association circuit held in Kissimmee.
Daytona 500: NASCAR race held at Daytona International Speedway.
March *Florida Strawberry Festival:* Held in Plant City (between Orlando and Tampa), this is a hugely popular event with country music, agricultural shows and fair rides.

Kissimmee Bluegrass Festival: Week-long toe-tapping music event.

Winter Park Sidewalk Arts Festival: long weekend of art, food, music and activities.

April *Central Florida Fair:* Equestrian shows, foot-stomping music and a carnival midway with rides and games at the Central Florida Fairgrounds.

Epcot International Flower & Garden Festival: garden and greenhouse tours, demonstrations and displays.

Kissimmee Jazz Fest: Top jazz artists, local musicians, crafts and food at Lakefront Park.

May *Florida Music Festival:* Three-day event with up-and-coming musicians, one of the best in the Southeast, held in downtown Orlando.

Zellwood Sweet Corn Festival: 200,000 corn on the cobs get consumed over the weekend at this family event.

June *Fiesta San Juan:* Annual celebration of Latin culture with food, music and dancing at Wet 'n Wild.

July *Lake Eola Fireworks over the Fountain:* Orlando celebrates the Fourth of July with games, activities and fireworks in Lake Eola Park.

September *Caribbean Festival and Italian Festival:* Themed weekends at Silver Springs with music, dancing, specialty dishes and festivities.

October *Walt Disney World® Golf Classic:* Top golfers gather for this annual PGA Tour event, played on the Palm and Magnolia courses.

Silver Spurs Rodeo: the cowboys are back in Kissimmee.

November *Cypress Gardens Mum (Chrysanthemum) Festival:* 3 million blooms in spectacular displays.

Annual Festival of the Masters: Art show at Downtown Disney®.

Fall Fiesta in the Park: Two-day arts and crafts show with 600 artisans, food and live entertainment in downtown Orlando's Lake Eola Park.

Festival of Lights at Silver Springs: Over 1 million twinkle lights, neon displays, choirs and a lighted boat parade, weekends late November–December.

December *Cypress Gardens Poinsettia Festival & Garden of Lights:* 400,000 lights and 40,000 poinsettias for Christmas.

Mickey's Very Merry Christmas Party: Celebrations at Magic Kingdom®.

Holiday Extravaganza: Strolling performers, live entertainment, spectacular fireworks and 20 tons of snow at Kissimmee Lakefront Park.

Orlando Citrus Parade: Marching bands and citrus floats made from thousands of pieces of grapefruit, oranges and tangerines.

Getting there

BY AIR

Orlando International Airport

9 miles (14.5km) to city center

🚌 N/A

🚍 45 minutes

🚗 30 minutes

Tampa International Airport

85 miles (137km) to city center

🚌 2 hours

🚍 2 hours

🚗 90 minutes

BY AIR

Orlando is a major domestic and an international airport. There are non-stop flights from about 70 different US destinations, and links to more than 100 cities worldwide. It is easily accessible and within 15 miles (24km) of major attractions, such as Walt Disney World® Resort, and downtown Orlando. Airport ☎ 407/825-2355.

The nearest alternative international gateway for scheduled flights is Tampa, 1½ hours from Orlando; several charter operators serve Orlando Sanford, 20 minutes away.

BY RAIL

Amtrak trains serve Orlando with four daily trains originating in New York, and Miami, also stopping at Winter Park and Sanford, north of the city, and Kissimmee near Walt Disney World® Resort. Amtrak offers an Auto Train overnight service with sleepers, which conveys passengers with their vehicles and runs daily between Lorton, Va and Sanford, Florida. For general information ☎ 1-800 872 7245 (toll free).

BY CAR

Interstate 4, or I-4, the area's main interstate highway, passes through Orlando and connects it with other parts of Florida. It runs roughly parallel to International Drive where many of the main attractions, hotels, restaurants and shops are located. US 192, also known as the Irlo Bronson Memorial Highway, intersects with I-4 and leads to Walt Disney World® Resort and many Kissimmee hotels.

BY BUS

Greyhound lines serve Orlando from many centers in the US: within the metropolitan area local buses provide a good service, notably Mears Transportation, which serves the airport and most of Orlando's main attractions and hotels. Greyhound bus ☎ 1-800 231 2222 (toll free); www.greyhound.com. For excursions around the area and to the major attractions, tour companies offer diverse itineraries or can customize trips for groups.

Getting around

PUBLIC TRANSPORT

Short-stay visitors can tackle Orlando without a car, though public transportation is pretty sketchy. Most hotels offer free shuttles to Walt Disney World® Resort, and Orlando's International Drive area has the inexpensive and efficient I-Ride trolley bus (8am–10:30pm) with scheduled stops every 20 minutes (see below).

Urban Transport Besides cab and limousine service to anywhere in the Greater Orlando area, the city's Lynx bus system provides economical public transportation around Orlando (☎ 407/841-8240, www.golynx.com). Bus stops are marked with a "paw" print of a Lynx cat.

The I-Ride Trolley serves International Drive, with stops every 20 minutes (☎ 407/354-5656; www.iridetrolley.com). The stops are marked "I-RIDE" at each Lynx bus stop. A second route, the Green Line trolley, serves the Major Boulevard business district, Universal Boulevard and South International Drive.

TAXIS

Cabs are plentiful in Orlando, but they are not accustomed to being hailed down in the street. Hotels are the best places to find a cab. If money is no object, limousine transportation can be easily arranged through your hotel's guest services desk.

DRIVING

● The Americans drive on the right side of the road.
● Seat belts must be worn by drivers and front-seat passengers. Children under four must use child safety seats; older children must use a safety seat or seat belt.
● Random breath-testing. Never drive under the influence of alcohol.

- Gas or gasoline (petrol) is cheaper in America than in Europe. It is sold in American gallons (five American gallons equal 18L), and comes in three grades, all unleaded. Many gas stations have automatic vending machines that accept notes and major credit cards.
- Speed limits, which are strictly enforced, are as follows:
  Interstate highways: 55–70mph/88–112kph
  Main roads: 55mph/88kph
  Urban roads: 20–30mph/32–48kph
- If you break down pull over, raise the hood (bonnet), switch on the hazard lights, and call the rental company or the breakdown number, which should be displayed on or near the dashboard. For added security, several major rental car agencies (including Alamo, Avis and Hertz) are now offering clients the option to rent an in-car cell phone.

CAR RENTAL

Rates are very competitive. Take an unlimited mileage deal, collision damage waiver and adequate (more than minimal) insurance. There is a surcharge on drivers under 25 and the minimum age is often 21 (sometimes 25). Expect to pay by credit card.

CONCESSIONS

Students with student ID cards and seniors age 55 and above can usually receive discounts on admission to museums and attractions. Most have reduced children's tickets (ages vary, but usually age 3–9) and free admission for children under 3.

Orlando's free Preferred Visitor Magicard gives discounts on attractions, accommodations, dining and transport. More information is available on www.orlandoinfo.com or from the tourist office

The theme parks have a host of multi-day and multi-park ticket options, so be sure and study them carefully and compare prices. You can sometimes (but not always) save money by booking online or in advance – at Universal Orlando tickets are cheapest by phone. Options include Disney's 7-day Magic Your Way base ticket, and Orlando Flex Tickets, which include unlimited admission for 14 consecutive days, available from participating parks. Four-park Flex tickets cover Universal Studios®, Islands of Adventure®, SeaWorld and Wet 'n Wild, five-park tickets also include Busch Gardens.

Being there

TOURIST OFFICES
Official Visitor Center
8723 International Drive, Gala
Center (cnr Austrian Row)
Orlando, Florida 32819
☎ 407/363-5872;
www.orlandoinfo.com
🕐 All year 8–7

Daytona Beach Area Convention and Visitors Center
Visitor Information Center, Daytona
USA, 1801 W International
Speedway Boulevard
☎ 386/253-8669 or 1-800 854
1234 or 1-866 644 9648
🕐 Daily 9–7

Florida's Space Coast Office of Tourism
8810 Astronaut Boulevard,
Cape Canaveral
☎ 321/637-5483 or

1-800 936 2326
Information desks at Kennedy
Space Center Visitor Complex;
www.space-coast.com

Kissimmee – St. Cloud Convention and Visitors Bureau
Visitor Information Center, 1925 E
Irlo Bronson Memorial
Highway/US192
☎ 407/847-5000 or 1-800 333 KISS
(5477); www.floridakiss.com
🕐 Mon–Fri 8–5

Tampa Bay Visitor Information Center
615 Channelside Drive
☎ 813/223-2752;
www.visittampabay.com
🕐 Daily 9:30–5

MONEY
The US dollar ($) is the official currency in the United States. Dollar bills come in 1,5, 10, 20, 50, 100 and 500 denominations. Note that all dollar bills are the same size and color – all greenbacks. One dollar is made up of 100 cents. Coins are of 1 cent (pennies), 5 cents (nickel), 10 cents (dime), 25 cents (quarter) and 1 dollar.

An unlimited amount of US dollars can be imported or exported, but amounts of over $10,000 must be reported to US Customs, as should similar amounts of gold. US dollars traveler's checks are accepted as cash in most places (not cabs) as are major credit cards.

TIPS/GRATUITIES

Yes ✓   No ✕

It is useful to have plenty of small notes

Hotels (chambermaid, doorman etc)	✓	$1
Restaurants (waiter, waitresses)	✓	15/20%
Bar Service	✓	15%
Cabs	✓	15%
Tour guides (discretionary)	✓	
Porters	✓	$1per bag
Lavatories	✕	

POSTAL AND INTERNET SERVICES

Post offices in Orlando are few and far between. Stamps from vending machines are sold at a 25 percent premium; it is best to buy them at your hotel. The international postcard rate is 75 cents. Post offices are usually open Monday to Friday 9am–5pm, but many hotels and major attractions provide a post office service out of hours.

Internet access is available at internet cafés, hotel rooms and business centers, and other locations such as Kinko's copying centers. Prices vary but are generally inexpensive. Many hotels and cafés have free WiFi access.

TELEPHONES

There are telephones in hotel lobbies, drug stores, restaurants, garages and at the roadside. A local call costs 25–50 cents. Buy cards for long distance calls from the Official Visitors Center, some pharmacies and grocery stores. Dial "0" for the operator. "Collect" means reverse the charges. Toll-free numbers usually begin with 1-800, 1-877 or 1-866.

International dialing codes

From Orlando (US) to:
UK: 011 44
Ireland: 011 353
Australia: 011 61
Germany: 011 49
Netherlands: 011 31
Spain: 011 34

Emergency telephone numbers

Police 911
Fire 911
Ambulance 911
Police (non emergency):
☎ 407/246-2414

EMBASSIES AND CONSULATES

UK ☎ 407/254-3300

Germany ☎ 202/298-4320
(Washington)

Netherlands ☎ 786/866-0480

Spain ☎ 305/446-5511 (Miami)

HEALTH ADVICE

Sun advice

By far the most common source of ill health in Florida is too much sun. Orlando in summer is very hot and humid and the sun is strong all year round. Use a sunscreen, wear a hat outdoors and ensure that everyone drinks plenty of fluids.

Drugs

Medicines can be bought at drug stores, certain drugs generally available elsewhere require a prescription in the US. Acetaminophen is the US equivalent of paracetamol. Take an insect repellent including Deet and cover up after dark, to avoid being bitten by mosquitoes.

Safe water

Restaurants usually provide a jug of iced water. Drinking unboiled water from taps is safe but not always very pleasant. Mineral water is inexpensive and readily available.

PERSONAL SAFETY

Orlando is not generally a dangerous place but to help prevent crime and accidents:

● Never open your hotel room door unless you know who is there. If in doubt call hotel security.

● Place valuables in a safety deposit box.

● Always lock your front and/or patio doors when in the room and when leaving. Use the safety chain/lock for security.

● When driving, keep all car doors locked.

● Never approach alligators, they can outrun a man.

ELECTRICITY

The power supply is 110/120 volts AC (60 cycles). Electrical sockets take two-prong, flat-pin plugs. Visitors should bring adaptors for their 3-pin and 2-round-pin plugs.

OPENING HOURS

● Shops ● Post Offices ● Pharmacies
● Banks ● Museums

There are two all-night pharmacies: Ekered Drugs, 908 Lee Road, and Walgreen Drug Store, International Drive (opposite Wet 'n Wild). Some shops in malls and on International Drive open until 9pm. Post offices are few and far between; hotels are usually helpful with postal matters. Banks, offices and post offices close on Saturday. Opening times of theme parks vary with seasonal demand. Opening times of museums vary; check with individual museum, some are closed on a Monday.

LANGUAGE

The official language of the USA is English. Spanish is also widely spoken. Certain words have a different meaning in American English, below are a few examples of such words and their British English equivalent.

ground floor	*first floor*	second floor	*third floor*
first floor	*second floor*	lift	*elevator*
I cent coin	*penny*	banknote	*bill*
5 cent coin	*nickel*	banknote (colloquial)	*greenback*
10 cent coin	*dime*	dollar (colloquial)	*buck*
25 cent coin	*quarter*	cashpoint	*automatic teller*
grilled	*broiled*	chips (potato)	*fries*
prawns	*shrimp*	crisps (potato)	*chips*
aubergine	*eggplant*	jam	*jelly*
courgette	*zucchini*	spirit	*liquor*
maize	*corn*	soft drink	*soda*

Best places to see

© Disney

1 Busch Gardens

www.buschgardens.com

The combination of exotic animals, thrilling roller-coasters, water rides and shows makes this one of Florida's top attractions.

Busch Gardens lies around 75 minutes' drive west of Orlando, in Tampa. Opened in 1959, it is a seasoned crowd-pleaser with pleasantly mature grounds shaded by trees and flowering shrubs. The overall plot is "Africa," with 10 themed areas such as Nairobi, Timbuktu and the Serengeti Plain; which incorporates the interactive Edge of Africa domain. It can be seen on the Serengeti Express Railway.

The 350-acre (141-ha) park houses one of the nation's premier zoos. There are more than 2,700 animals from over 300 species wandering the grassland enclosures of the Serengeti Plain, inhabiting the rocks and waterfalls of the Great Ape Domain and featured in other displays such as the Bird Gardens. Busch Gardens plays a significant role in breeding and conserving endangered species and many of the zoo's latest additions are proudly displayed in the Nairobi Animal Nursery.

But animals are by no means all the park has to offer: roller-coaster fans are also in for a big treat. Check out the duelling, double wooden roller-coaster Gwazi and Montu, one of the tallest and longest inverted coasters in the world. The Kumba ride remains among the largest and fastest steel

roller-coasters in existence, and assorted
water rides provide varying degrees of
thrills and spills, plus a chance to cool off in
the Florida sunshine.

Small children are particularly well catered-for
here. In addition to the animal attractions, there is
the interactive Land of the Dragons play area, and
colorful "Lion King" style show in the Moroccan
Palace Theater. Strollers are available for rental in
the Morocco district and there is a full baby-
changing and nursing area in Land of the Dragons.

See also ➤ 76–81.

➕ 134 E1 (off map) ✉ Busch Boulevard, Tampa (75 miles/
121km west of Orlando via I-4 West and I-75 North to
Fowler Avenue/Exit 265) ☎ 813/987-5082 or 1-888 800
5447 ⏰ Daily 10–6 (extended summer and hols) 💵 Very
expensive 🍴 Refreshment stops throughout park, plus the
full-service Crown Colony Restaurant (Crown Colony) ($–$$)
❓ Check daily schedules for show times

2 Cypress Gardens Adventure Park

www.cypressgardens.com

Florida's first theme park remains faithful to its botanical origins and is famous for its four annual flower festivals.

Sloping gently down to the shores of Lake Eloise, near Winter Haven, a 45-minute drive south of Orlando, Cypress Gardens was originally laid out in the 1930s along the swampy water's edge, shaded by giant cypress trees. The park has expanded considerably since, covering more than 220 acres (89ha), and offers a variety of shows, shopping, dining and animal attractions in addition to the carefully manicured gardens, eye-catching topiary and other horticultural exhibits.

For plant-lovers, the lush Botanical Gardens

remain the highlight of a visit. Shaded brick paths meander through dense tropical plantings of heliconias and bromeliads, cascades of brilliantly colored bougainvillea and forests of bamboo.

But flower power aside, Cypress Gardens takes pride in its water-ski revues on the lake, and the 153-ft (47-m) high Island in the Sky revolving observatory. At its foot, Jubilee Junction houses snack stops, restaurants and shops.

Other attractions concentrate on the wonders of the natural world, with the Wings of Wonder Butterfly Conservatory and the Nature's Way area featuring animal enclosures and a wooden boardwalk area on the lake. A recent addition is a kid-pleasing assortment of amusement rides: tilt-a-whirls, roller coasters, flume rides, and other cars and cages that flip, spin and roll. To be sure, however, this is still a botanical garden at heart and a good place to experience an old-fashioned Florida attraction.

✚ 134 F2 ✉ SR540 West 4 miles (6.5km) east of Winter Haven, off US27, 22 miles (35km) south of I-4 ☎ 863/324-2111 ◷ Daily 10–6 (closing times vary) ⑪ Aunt Julie's Country Kitchen ($–$$$); Backwater Bill's BBQ ($); Sandra Dee's Diner ($); Village Fare Food Court ($); assorted snack and refreshment stops ($) ⑫ Very expensive

3 Discovery Cove

www.discoverycove.com

Swim with dolphins, rays and thousands of tropical fish then laze on the sand at this beach paradise created in landlocked Orlando.

To swim with dolphins is a cherished dream for millions, so it should come as no surprise that somebody in Orlando came up with the brilliant idea of creating a theme park where this particular dream can come true. Sister to the world-famous SeaWorld Orlando (➤ 38–39) theme park across the road (and Busch Gardens in Tampa, ➤ 28–29, 76–81). Unlike other theme parks, which rely on a high turnover of guests, Discovery Cove aims for exclusivity. Admission is by advance reservation only and limited to 1,000 guests per day ensuring the park is never over-run and the all-important dolphin-swim program is not compromised.

As well as the 45-minute dolphin swim guests can snorkel among thousands of tropical reef fish from 90 different species in a coral reef setting, while sharks and barracudas patrol just a few inches away behind plexiglass safety panels. While at Ray Lagoon they can wade into a world of sleek and mysterious rays as dozens of southern and cownose stingrays, which can grow up to 4ft (1.25m) across, glide past to be touched and fed little snacks. For those looking to relax there is plenty of space on the sandy beaches around the resort-style swimming pool, or guests can take a gentle meander down Tropical River, which flows past sunken ruins and hidden grottoes, waterfalls and beaches to the 12,000-sq ft (1,115-sq m) aviary. For an additional fee, you can also get behind the scenes. The park offers a Trainer for a Day program for just 12 guests a day where you can work side-by-side with animal experts.

A day at Discovery Cove may seem like a very expensive option (about $275), but keep in mind that everything is included from towel and snorkel to wetsuit, and you'll have a very nice lunch that enhances your day.

✠ 142 C4 ✉ 6000 Discovery Cove Way (1-4/Exit 71 or 72) ☎ 407/370-1280 or 1-877 434 7268 🕓 Daily 8–5:30 ✋ Very expensive; a reduced package is available for children 3–5 and guests who do not take part in the dolphin swim 🍴 Breakfast and lunch in the Laguna Grill is included in the admission price; the Oasis snack cabanas ($) serve refreshments 🚌 I-Ride, Lynx #42 ❓ The hands-on Trainer for a Day program is available for up to 12 guests a day. Reservations essential

4 Harry P. Leu Gardens

www.leugardens.org

Three miles (5km) of walkways take you through a series of beautiful themed gardens created by Harry Leu and his wife.

Sloping down to the shores of Lake Rowena, these lovely 50-acre (20-ha) gardens provide a soothing escape from the hustle and bustle. They were originally laid out by local businessman Harry P. Leu and his wife, who purchased the property in 1936 and lived in historic Leu House, a much-enlarged pioneer home that now houses a museum.

Near the entrance, the lush Ravine Garden leads down to a boardwalk and a gazebo that overlooks the lake. Coots and ducks potter about in the lake's waters and the occasional wild alligator lurks here. To the west of the property, mature southern magnolias and spreading live oaks shade the camellia woods, which can be seen at their best during the October to March flowering season. The Leus planted more than 2,000 camellia specimens here, and their collection is considered to be one of the finest in the eastern US.

The floral centerpiece is the Rose Garden, a popular setting for open-air weddings among the 1,000 scented rose bushes. Close by, Leu House is open for regular tours. In the far corner of the gardens, the Display Greenhouse is a riot of hothouse orchids, tropical gingers, anthuriums, heliconias and ferns.

➕ 139 A6 ✉ 1920 N Forest Avenue ☎ 407/246-2620
🕐 Daily 9–5 except Christmas Day. Leu House tours daily 10–3:30 (last tour) ✋ Inexpensive

5 Kennedy Space Center

www.kennedyspacecenter.com

Tours, films, rockets and space hardware bring the American space program to life at NASA's Florida space launch facility.

The Kennedy Space Center Visitor Complex is the gateway to Launch Complex 39, where space shuttles will one day again blast off into orbit, and where *Apollo 11* set off on its ground-breaking journey to deliver the first man to walk on the moon in 1969. A visit to the Space Center offers a terrific opportunity to delve into the history of the US space program, experience a nail-biting re-creation of the countdown to blast off and get a behind-the-scenes view of past and future space technology.

The very first rockets launched from Cape Canaveral were long-range guided missiles fired from Cape Canaveral Air Force Station in the early 1950s. NASA, the National Aeronautics and Space Administration established in 1958 to carry out the peaceful exploration and use of space, later used the site to prepare and launch science satellites and the manned and unmanned flights of the early Mercury and Gemini programs. In 1964, NASA transferred operations to Launch Complex 39, at Merritt Island, which was designed to handle the Apollo-Saturn V program. The first

launch from the Kennedy
Space Center was the
Apollo 8 mission
December 1968.

Today, bus tours offer
views of the shuttle launch
pads, the gargantuan
Vehicle Assembly Building
(VAB) and make a stop at
the spectacular $37-million
Apollo/Saturn V Center,
which features an actual,
unused, *Saturn V* rocket.
Families with small
children will find a half-day
visit long enough. But do
save time to watch at least
one IMAX movie (included
in admission).
"Magnificent Desolation:
Walking on the Moon 3-D"
and "Space Station 3-D"
are inspiring.

✠ 135 C8 ✉ SR405, Merritt
Island (Bee Line Expressway/
SR528 toll road east from
Orlando) ☎ 321/449-4444
or 321/454-4198 TDD
🕐 Daily 9–dusk 🖐 Expensive
🍴 Mila's ($–$$); cafés and
concessions ($) ❓ Bus
tours depart regularly (allow
2.5 hours)

SeaWorld Orlando

www.seaworld.com

Shamu, the killer whale, star of SeaWorld, heads up an all-star cast at the world's most popular sea life park.

Laid out over an action-packed 200-acre (81-ha) site, SeaWorld provides a full day's itinerary of shows and marine encounters in the best theme park tradition. The stars of the shows are almost exclusively of the finned or flippered variety and their virtuoso performances (coaxed by the strategic deployment of fish) are a source of continuous amazement and delight to packed audiences. Though SeaWorld can get very busy, its built-in advantage over other traditional parks is the scarcity of rides, so there are few long lines.

Shamu shows, especially the evening version – Shamu Rocks America – are hugely popular and performances in the Whale & Dolphin Stadium and the Sea Lion & Otter Stadium are a must. The Penguin Encounter (with real snow) should not be missed, and anybody who has never seen a manatee should rectify this immediately at Manatees: The Last Generation?

SeaWorld pushes its role as a significant animal rescue, conservation and research facility. There are several entertaining and educational behind-the-scenes tours for interested guests as well as summer camp adventures. For an even more interactive experience, SeaWorld's sister park, Discovery Cove, invites guests to swim with bottlenose dolphins and tropical fish (► 32–33). See also ► 59–64.

➕ 142 C4 ✉ 7007 SeaWorld Drive, Orlando (I-4/Exit 71 or 72 ☎ 407/351-3600 or 1-800 432 1178 🕐 Daily 9–7 (extended summer and hols) 💷 Very expensive. There is a 10 percent discount for ticket purchases made over the internet, or as part of the 4- and 5-Park Orlando Flex Tickets 🍴 Makahiki Luau, Dine With Shamu, Sharks Underwater Grill ($$$), reservations ☎ 1-800 327 2424. Also assorted cafés, snack, BBQ and sandwich shops 🚌 I-Ride, Lynx #42

7 Silver Springs

www.silversprings.com

Boat trips, jeep safaris, animal encounters and popular music shows are all part of the deal at "Florida's Original Attraction."

In 1878, Silver Springs entrepreneur Hullam Jones had a brainwave. He installed a glass viewing box in the flat bottom of a dugout canoe and invented the glass-bottomed boat tour, hence this popular nature park's claim to being the Sunshine State's first tourist attraction.

More than a century on, the glass-bottomed boat rides are as popular as ever, creating a window into an underwater world teeming with fish, turtles, crustaceans and ancient fossils at the head of the world's largest artesian spring formation. You can also enjoy the Lost River Voyage that plies the unspoilt Silver River, with a stop at a wildlife rescue outpost; or a Jungle Cruise on Fort King Waterway, where non-native animals look on. Jeep safaris also do the jungle thing, four-wheeling through a 35-acre (14-ha) Florida jungle, with specially designed animal habitats like Big Gator Lagoon.

Showtime at Silver Springs brings on the bugs and the creepy-crawlies at Creature Feature, an alarmingly up-close look at spiders and scorpions, toads and giant Madagascan hissing cockroaches. For something a little more wholesome, watch domestic cats and dogs performing tricks at the Amazing Pets displays. The park also attracts popular music acts for its annual weekend Concert Series (included with admission) starting in March.

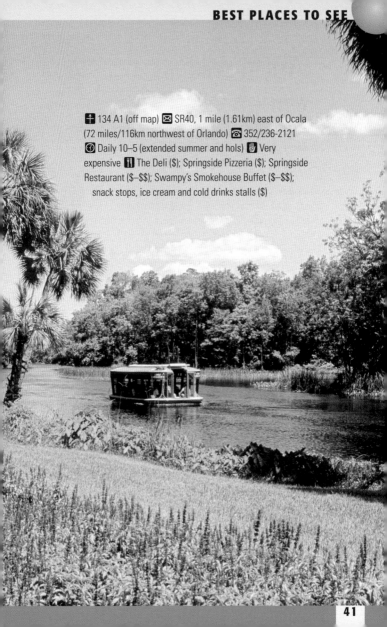

✚ 134 A1 (off map) ✉ SR40, 1 mile (1.61km) east of Ocala (72 miles/116km northwest of Orlando) ☎ 352/236-2121 ◔ Daily 10–5 (extended summer and hols) 💵 Very expensive 🍴 The Deli ($); Springside Pizzeria ($); Springside Restaurant ($–$$); Swampy's Smokehouse Buffet ($–$$); snack stops, ice cream and cold drinks stalls ($)

8 Wet 'n Wild

www.wetnwildorlando.com

If the beach is too far, Wet 'n Wild is a perfect – and in some ways much more exciting – alternative.

When it opened in 1977, Wet 'n Wild set the standard for the elaborate water park. There was more than simply a few slides here; there were twisting, barreling, churning rapids as well as innovative watery rides, wide beaches, a surf lagoon, restaurants, picnic areas and a lazy river. The park, located on International Drive, is hugely popular from April to October, with the peak season running from June through August.

You will be astonished at the ingenuity that has gone into creating heart-stopping thrill rides. For instance, the Black Hole sends you shooting 500ft (152m) down a spinning, twisting, dark tunnel, forced through by a gusher of water. Der Stuka is one of the highest, fastest waterslides in the world. One of the scariest attractions is Bomb Bay. Step into a large enclosed cylinder, cross your arms and legs, and then the floor below you drops out to send you sliding on a 76-ft (23-m) vertical free fall before you slip into a curve to slow your descent. Kids are catered to with a separate area featuring thrilling kid-sized rides and attractions.

You don't have to be a thrillseeker to enjoy Wet 'n Wild; there are plenty of more peaceful offerings. You can bring picnic lunches and coolers with food into the park, the pools are heated, as many as 400 lifeguards are on duty in peak season, and this is one of the rare water parks opened year-round.

✚ 137 F5 ✉ 6200 International Drive (1–4/Exit 75AB) ☎ 407/351-1800 or 1-800 992 WILD (9453) 🕐 Daily 10–5 (extending 9–9 or later in summer) ✋ Very expensive 🍴 Surf Grill ($–$$); Bubba's BBQ & Chicken ($–$$); Manny's Pizza & Subs ($–$$); Cookies & Cones ($) 🚌 I-Ride, Lynx 42

9 Walt Disney World® Resort

www.disneyworld.com

This is the big one: Walt Disney's Florida showcase put Orlando on the map and has become a legend in its own short lifetime.

Walt Disney World® Resort is the largest and most famous theme park resort in the world. Its 27,500-acre (11,134-ha) site is twice the size of Manhattan, and although only a small portion of this has been developed to date, it has four major theme parks: Magic Kingdom®, Epcot®, Disney's Hollywood Studios (formerly Disney-MGM Studios) and Disney's Animal Kingdom® Park, plus two water parks, a nightclub area within the huge lakefront Downtown Disney® shopping, dining and entertainment district, themed resorts, gardens, golf courses and a professional sports complex.

Walt Disney opened his first theme park in Anaheim, California, in 1955. Disneyland, the prototype for the Magic Kingdom® (which now flourishes in Japan, France and Hong Kong, as well as Florida) was a huge success, but Disney was unable to control the explosion of hotels that popped up around the site and prevented him from expanding the park. Instead, he looked for alternative spots and was drawn to Orlando for its climate, communications links and vast tracts of cheap farmland, which

© Disney

© Disney

he began to purchase in secret during 1964. With 27,500 acres (11,134ha) in the bag at a cost of about $5.5 million, Disney announced his plans to create "a complete vacation environment".

Disney died in 1966 without seeing his Florida vision completed. But The Walt Disney Company did him proud, producing Magic Kingdom® in Disneyland's image. This opened in 1971, followed by Epcot® in 1982, then Disney-MGM Studios was rushed out in 1989, months ahead of Universal Studios' mammoth Florida facility (➤ 46–47). Now Central Florida's animal-orientated parks are feeling the pinch as Disney's Animal Kingdom® Park exercises its powerful Disney appeal on the public.

"Doing Disney" is quite an undertaking. Take a tip from the repeat visitors who plan their itineraries with almost military precision, zero in on the best rides and avoid the restaurants at peak times. Never plan on doing more than one park a day, and if you are visiting all four parks include at least one rest day. See also ➤ 101–129.

➕ 140 D4 ✉ Walt Disney World® Resort, Lake Buena Vista (US 192 and several exits off I-4, 20 miles/32km south of Orlando) ☎ 407/824-4321 🕐 Check current schedules ✋ Very expensive 🚌 Free shuttle bus services from many Orlando/Kissimmee hotels ❓ Details of daily parades, showtimes and nighttime displays are printed in current park guides. Tickets are available on a one-day, one-park basis. For longer stay guests, a choice of multi-day passes offer greater flexibility and savings. They cover unlimited admission to any combination of theme parks, WDW Resort transportation, and limited admission to other Disney attractions. Unused days expire 14 days after activation

10 Universal Orlando® Resort

www.universalorlando.com

Blockbuster rides, shows and attractions recreate movie magic and comic strip heroes at Universal's two Florida theme parks.

Disney may have greater worldwide recognition, but for many visitors to Orlando – particularly adult and teenage thrillseekers – Universal delivers a more exciting theme park experience. The original, movie-orientated, Universal Studios® Florida theme park opened in 1990, sharing a site with the largest working movie and television production facility outside Hollywood. It soon developed a worldwide reputation for innovative, state-of-the-art thrill rides. Recently the excellent and extremely popular Shrek 4-D™, Revenge of the Mummy℠ – The Ride and newly opened Simpsons ride have added three brand new reasons to visit Universal.

In 1999, Universal Studios® Florida metamorphosed into Universal Orlando® Resort, a complete resort destination with on-site hotels, the 30-acre (12-ha) Universal CityWalk® shopping, dining and entertainment complex, and a second theme park, Universal's Islands of Adventure®. Adrenaline junkies are in for a treat at Islands of Adventure®, which styles its roller-coaster and thrill rides after Marvel comic book heroes such as Spider-Man, Doctor Doom and the Incredible Hulk. A further range of rides and shows features the likes of Sinbad the Sailor, Jurassic Park's dinosaurs and children's favorites Dr. Seuss and Popeye.

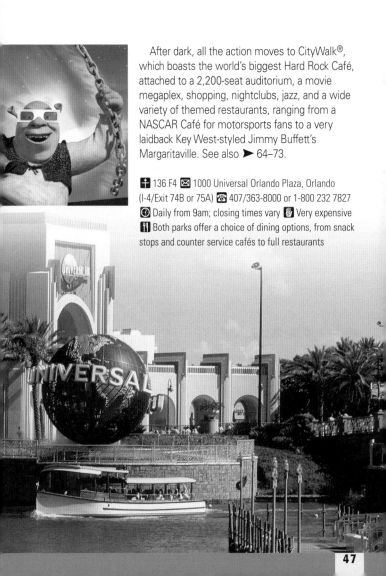

After dark, all the action moves to CityWalk®, which boasts the world's biggest Hard Rock Café, attached to a 2,200-seat auditorium, a movie megaplex, shopping, nightclubs, jazz, and a wide variety of themed restaurants, ranging from a NASCAR Café for motorsports fans to a very laidback Key West-styled Jimmy Buffett's Margaritaville. See also ➤ 64–73.

✚ 136 F4 ✉ 1000 Universal Orlando Plaza, Orlando (I-4/Exit 74B or 75A) ☎ 407/363-8000 or 1-800 232 7827 🕐 Daily from 9am; closing times vary ✋ Very expensive 🍴 Both parks offer a choice of dining options, from snack stops and counter service cafés to full restaurants

Exploring

In the 1930s, traffic signals in downtown Orlando wore a sign admonishing drivers to be quiet. There were fresh fruit juice stands on the sidewalk and the city resembled "a great, cultivated park." Since Orlando has become synonymous with theme parks, it is generally assumed to be a loud, brash place. Living in the shadow of the Mouse has certainly brought radical changes. The mini-Manhattan of the downtown district is bounded by highways, and the sky is busy with jets coming to and going from the international airport. But the city of Orlando has not succumbed entirely to the trappings of the tourist industry. There are pockets of greenery in Lake Eola and Harry P. Leu Gardens, and recent developments have included the renovated historic district around Downtown, the Orlando Science Center and its satellite art and history museums, and the palatial Orange County Convention Center.

Orlando

Orlando's untidy outline sprawls either side of I-4, the fast interstate highway that slices diagonally across Central Florida from Tampa on the Gulf of Mexico to Daytona on the Atlantic Coast.

The city has extended steadily southwest towards Walt Disney World® Resort and Kissimmee, and most visitors who stay in Orlando are based south of the city in the International Drive resort area. SeaWorld, Discovery Cove and Universal Orlando are just off I-Drive (as International Drive is familiarly called), which is served by the I-Ride trolley.

It may come as a suprise to the vast majority of visitors who never venture beyond the distinctly touristy environs of I-Drive and the major theme parks, but Orlando does have more to offer than the well-traveled strip of hotels, motels, discount malls and smaller attractions that constitute the city's main resort area.

DISCOVERY COVE

Best places to see, ➤ 32–33.

GATORLAND

Southeast of Orlando, on the border with Kissimmee, a pair of giant alligator jaws forms the entrance to this classic Florida attraction. Hundreds of captive "gators" occupy various pens and pools. There are alligator shows, alligator meals (try Gator Nuggets in Pearl's Smokehouse), and alligator products, such as wallets, boots and handbags, on sale in the gift shop. Other Gatorland residents include Florida crocodiles and caymans, native snapping and soft-shell turtles, and snake displays feature venomous rattlesnakes and cottonmouth moccasins.

A highlight is the 2,000-ft (610-m) long marshland boardwalk edging a cypress swamp. This is a native habitat alligator breeding ground and a great birdwatching spot. In spring, snowy egrets construct their nests within a few feet of passers-by, and there are great and little blue herons, pigeon-sized little green herons and dozens of other wading birds.

www.gatorland.com

➕ 143 F7 ✉ 14501 S Orange Blossom Trail ☎ 407/855-5496 or 1-800 393 5297 🕐 Daily 9am–dusk 💂 Expensive 🍴 Pearl's Smokehouse ($)

HARRY P. LEU GARDENS

Best places to see, ➤ 34–35.

HERITAGE SQUARE

A focus for downtown Orlando, the Heritage Square development
has been designed to symbolize "the heart of the community."
This is the site where the city's early pioneers would have plotted
out the land and planned its development. The old Orange County
Courthouse is here, which houses the Orange County Regional
History Center (► 55), and the almost 2-acre (1-ha) park and plaza
has been attractively landscaped with native trees, plants and
Floridian-inspired landmarks as well as a pop-jet fountain that is a
magnet for children.

🚩 139 B5 ⊠ Central Boulevard at Magnolia Avenue (I-4 to exit 82C/
Anderson Street)

MENNELLO MUSEUM

Florida's only folk art museum is a
delightful find for fans of the genre. The
works of Earl Cunningham (1893–1977)
form the basis of the collections courtesy
of Florida collectors Michael and Marilyn
Mennello, who are donating 44 of
Cunningham's works to the museum
over 13 years. Cunningham, who could
list chicken farmer, seaman and junk
dealer among his former careers, favored
"historical-fantasy" themes and his
colorful palette adapts superbly to
exuberant depictions of typically Floridian
scenes from florious technicolor sunsets
and native birdlife to Seminole villages,
and lively marine paintings featuring his
favorite early 20th-century schooners.
The museum also hosts regular visiting
exhibitions of modern and antique
paintings and sculpture.

www.mennellomuseum.org
✚ 139 A5 ✉ 900 E Princeton Street (I-4 to exit 85) ☎ 407/246-4278
🕐 Tue–Sat 10:30–4:30, Sun 12–4:30 ✋ Inexpensive

ORANGE COUNTY REGIONAL HISTORY CENTER

Unfortunately, many visitors believe Florida was discovered by Walt Disney. At this first-class museum, historians try to set the record straight by focusing on the people and society that existed in the pre-theme park years. In the handsomely restored 1927 Orange County Courthouse, the Center recalls Central Florida history through imaginative audio and visual presentations as well as hands-on exhibits. You are greeted by The Dome, a three-dimensional showcase for Florida icons, followed by an orientation experience. Suitably immersed in local lore, exhibits whisk you back in time to the Paleo-Indian era and a Timucuan village, the arrival of the Spanish explorers, a pioneer Cracker homestead, and the Roaring 20s when Tin Can tourists in Model-T Fords descended on Florida in their thousands.

www.thehistorycenter.org
✚ 139 B5 ✉ One Heritage Square, 65 E Central Boulevard (I-4 to Exit 82C/Anderson Street) ☎ 407/836-8500 or 1-800 965 2030 🕐 Mon–Sat 10–5, Sun 12–5 ✋ Inexpensive

ORLANDO MUSEUM OF ART

The museum invites tourists to experience Orlando's cultural side and often hosts touring exhibitions, so check current schedules. If the permanent collections are on show, visitors will be rewarded with a notable collection of pre-Columbian art – some 250 pieces dating from around 1200BC to AD1500 – plus works by leading 19th- to 20th-century American artists and African art exhibits.
www.omart.org

✛ 139 A5 ✉ Loch Haven Park, 2416 North Mills Avenue at E Princeton Street (I-4/Exit 85) ☎ 407/896-4231 ◷ Tue–Fri 10–4, Sat–Sun 12–4
💵 Moderate

ORLANDO SCIENCE CENTER

Topped by a distinctive silver observatory dome, Orlando's impressive Science Center opened its doors in 1997. The exhibits are laid out over four levels and include dozens of interactive displays and hands-on educational games designed to appeal to children of all ages – and not a few adults as well.

On ground level, the NatureWorks Florida habitat section combines models and living exhibits such as turtles, baby alligators and a reef tank, and there is the excellent KidsTown early learning area for 8s and under. On Levels 2, 3 and 4, more elaborate and sophisticated exhibits tackle the basics of physics, mathematics, applied technologies and human biology in comprehensible and entertaining style. Movie moguls should definitely see the TechWorks exhibit on Level 4, which explores the behind-the-scenes tricks of the movie trade.

In addition, there are daily science-orientated shows in the Darden Adventure Theater and the Digistar Planetarium, and large format film presentations in the CineDome, which boasts a massive 8,000sq-ft (732sq-m) IMAX screen. On Friday and Saturday nights, while the CineDome features 3-D laser light shows, the Observatory welcomes stargazers.

www.osc.org

🏁 139 A5 ✉ 777 E Princeton Street (I-4/Exit 85) ☎ 407/514-2000 or 1-888 672 4386 🕑 Sun–Thu 10–6, Fri–Sat 10–9 💷 Moderate 🍴 OSC Cafe ($)

RIPLEY'S BELIEVE IT OR NOT!
ORLANDO ODDITORIUM

A whacky, lop-sided building tipping down an imaginary sinkhole, a hologram greeting from the long-dead Robert L Ripley and hundreds of curious, eccentric and downright bizarre exhibits add up to a fairly unbelievable attraction. Robert Ripley was a connoisseur of oddities. Traveling extensively in the 1920s and 1930s, he amassed enough material to stock more than a dozen "museums" of this type worldwide. Typical exhibits include a Mona Lisa made from 1,426 squares of toast and a three-quarter scale model of a 1907 Rolls Royce Silver Ghost made out of 1,016,711 matchsticks and 63 pints of glue.

✚ 142 B4 ✉ 8201 International Drive ☎ 407/345-0501 or 1-800 998 4418 ◷ Daily 9am–1am ✋ Expensive ⊟ I-Ride, Lynx #42

SEAWORLD ORLANDO

SeaWorld's well-balanced combination of sights and shows is a proven winner. Unlike some parks, where the shows are incidental to the main action, here they are an intrinsic ingredient, and the rest of the attractions – plus behind-the-scenes tours – can be fitted in as visitors make their way around the many and various show stadiums.

Unusual dining options in the park include Dine with Shamu and the classy Sharks Underwater Grill. Sunset reveals another side of SeaWorld, with nightly laser and fireworks displays and the Makahiki Luau Dinner and Show. Below is a list of highlights; see also ➤ 38–39.

Sea Lion and Otter Stadium

Sea lions, otters and lumbering walruses are incorporated in the melodramatic swashbuckling tale, "Clyde and Seamore Take Pirate Island." Weaving cute tricks into the story highlights the animal attraction.

Journey to Atlantis

Rickety Greek fishing boats transport guests on a sightseeing trip to the newly risen City of Atlantis when disaster strikes and a high-speed water ride with special effects ensues.

Key West at SeaWorld

A Florida Keys themed area, with a tropical atmosphere and street performers. The centerpiece is 2-acre (1-ha) Dolphin Cove, a lagoon habitat for Atlantic bottlenose dolphins adjacent to the Whale & Dolphin Stadium. Rescued turtles bask on the rocks of Turtle Point, visitors can feed and pet captive stingrays in the Stingray Lagoon, and there are nightly festivities in Sunset Square.

Kraken

More thrills aboard a mega sea serpent-styled roller-coaster.

Manatee Rescue

A distant aquatic relative of the elephant, the manatee is now a seriously endangered species. There may be fewer than 2,000 of these giant Florida sea cows left in the wild. All the manatees in this SeaWorld exhibit are rescued and will be returned to the wild if possible.

Pacific Point Preserve
California sea lions, harbor seals and South American fur seals occupy this rocky northern Pacific coast re-creation, complete with wave machine.

Penguin Encounter
Some 200 enchanting Antarctic penguins and their Arctic cousins, the alcids (better known as puffins and mures), inhabit these icy confines.

Shamu Adventure
An introduction to the world of the killer whale hosted by animal expert Jack Hanna. Makes a good preface to the Shamu stadium shows.

Shamu's Happy Harbor
Play area for small children with climbing apparatus, radio-controlled boats, a sandpit and face-painting activities.

Terrors of the Deep
Scene-setting, spooky music and eerie lighting accompany these aquariums full of lurking moray eels, 28-mph (45-kph) barracudas and highly toxic puffer fish. Ride the perspex tunnel through the 660,000-gal shark tank, or get really up close and personal with the park's daring interaction program, Sharks Deep Dive, and don a wetsuit for a ride through the habitat in a shark cage.

Wild Arctic

A simulated helicopter ride transports visitors to an Arctic base station for close encounters with polar bears, beluga whales and walruses.

www.seaworld.com

✚ 142 C4 ✉ 7007 SeaWorld Drive, Orlando (I-4/Exit 71 or72) ☎ 407/351-3600 or 1-800 432 1178 ◷ Daily 9–7 (extended summer and hols) ✋ Orlando FlexTickets offer reduced rates and flexibility. Available from participating parks, 4-Park tickets provide unlimited admission to SeaWorld Orlando, Universal Orlando and Wet 'n Wild. 5-Park tickets include Busch Gardens in Tampa ⊪ Several restaurants and snack stops. Reservations for Dine With Shamu, Sharks Underwater Grill and Makahiki Luau should be made in advance on ☎ 1-800 327 2424 🚌 I-Ride, Lynx #42 ❓ Guided tours of Terrors of the Deep, Wild Arctic and the animal rescue and research facility can be made at the Guided Tours counter near the entrance. For Sharks Deep Dive, the Beluga Interaction Program, Marine Mammal Keeper plus the guided Adventure Express Tour of the park, advance reservations are recommended, ☎ 1-800 432 1178 (press 5)

UNIVERSAL ORLANDO® RESORT

See pages 46–47 and information under Universal Studios® and Universal's Islands of Adventure®.

UNIVERSAL STUDIOS®

It would be a mistake to assume that if you have done Disney's Hollywood Studios (➤ 109–111) you should skip this. The Universal experience is more ride-orientated than its Disney rival and the attractive layout is a definite plus. The most popular shows on the Universal lot include the Beetlejuice's Graveyard Revue™; Blues

Brothers® soul-style entertainment; and Animal Actors On Location!™ showcasing talented animals. Below is a list of highlights.

Earthquake®
It is a short step off the San Francisco street set to this subway journey from hell. Experience an 8.3 on the Richter Scale, as portrayed in the classic 1974 disaster movie *Earthquake*.

ET Adventure®
A gentle ride over 3,340 miniature buildings aboard flying bicycles with ET in a basket on the front handlebars. A ride that appeals to younger children.

Jaws®
Set amid the seaside architecture and artfully arranged lobster pots of a re-created fishing village, Captain Jake's Amity Boat Tours embark for a wholly expected watery encounter with the glistening jaws of Universal's famous 32-ft (10-m), three-ton mechanical great white shark. The steel-and-fibreglass shark moves at speeds of up to 20ft (6m) per second, with a thrust power equal to a 727 jet engine. Passengers still love it, and this is a particularly attractive corner of the park.

Jimmy Neutron's Nicktoon Blast™
A Nickelodeon children's TV animated favorite, Jimmy has leapt from small to large screen and now merits his very own theme park ride. Bucket along in the boy genius' Rocket Pod to rescue the world from evil egg-shaped Yokian aliens.

MEN IN BLACK™ Alien Attack™
An interactive chase through the streets of New York in hot pursuit of invading aliens. Terrific techno-futuristic styling, wild maneuvres and weapons that rack up your score from hero to loser.

Revenge of the Mummy℠ – The Ride

The horrors and highlights of the popular Brendan Fraser film are presented here, within the frightening passages of a darkened pyramid. Super scary effects and a roller coaster race in the dark have made this a highlight.

Shrek 4-D™

An adventure for the swamp-dwelling ogre and his lovely bride, Princess Fiona. Share the couple's honeymoon on 4-D "Ogrevision" complete with multi-sensory effects (including alarming pneumatic seats). The entertaining pre-show catches up non-fans on the storyline, and the show itself is a nice, fast-paced 3-D bridge between the original movie and its sequel.

The Simpsons

Stars of the small screen, then the big screen and now a theme park ride – this new attraction is set to become a classic. Head there early in the day to avoid the queues.

Terminator 2®: 3-D Battle Across Time

The world's first 3-D virtual adventure, "T2:3-D" (to aficionados) reunited the *Terminator 2* team to produce the most expensive film, frame for frame, ever made: $24 million for 12 minutes. The audience is transported into an apocalyptic world, showered with 3-D flying debris and whirlygig mini-hunter pocket gunships, and menaced by the flexi-steel pincers of the re-generating T-1,000,000. Fantastic effects: not to be missed, however long the line.

Twister… Ride It Out®

Lifted from the blockbuster movie, this multi-million dollar tornado encounter is not for the faint-hearted. Brave a five-story-high cyclone, complete with torrential rain and howling winds.

Universal Horror Make-Up Show

After seeing props and make-up effects from classic horror films, you enter a theater where a host and a special effects expert deliver a side-splittingly fun and funny presentation on make-up and movie tricks.

Woody Woodpecker's KidZone®

A child-friendly zone of scaled down rides, adventure play areas and shows to delight the very young. Teeny thrills on Woody Woodpecker's Nuthouse Coaster, sing-a-long with the dinky dinosaurs in A Day In The Park With Barney, let off steam in Fievel's Playland or cool down amongst the water jets of the interactive Curious George Goes to Town play area.

www.universalorlando.com

✚ 136 E4 ✉ 1000 Universal Plaza, Orlando (I-4/Exit 74B or 75A) ☎ 407/363-8000 or 1-888 322 5537 🕐 Daily from 9am; closing times vary 💰 Very expensive. Orlando FlexTickets offer reduced rates and flexibility. Available from participating parks, 4-Park tickets provide unlimited admission to SeaWorld Orlando, Universal Studios® Escape and Wet 'n Wild over 14 consecutive days. 5-Park tickets include Busch Gardens in Tampa. For further information ☎ 1-800 224 3838 🍴 Both parks offer a choice of dining options from snack stops and counter-service cafés to full-service restaurants

ISLANDS OF ADVENTURE®

Universal employed the creative genius of movie director Steven Spielberg to help bring favorite comic strip characters and mythical legends to life in their second Florida theme park. Islands of Adventure® claims to be the most technologically advanced theme park in the world combining a host of hair-raising rides and boldly drawn, imaginative surroundings. Unlike its sister park, where the rides and attractions bear little relation to the stylized districts they inhabit, Islands of Adventure® has five distinctively themed "islands" linked by footbridges and water transportation from the Port of Entry. The park's highlights are listed island-by-island below.

Jurassic Park®

A lushly landscaped "island" with a familiar theme based on Spielberg's blockbuster movie. Enjoy an overview of the district from the Pteranodon Flyers aerial runway; get up close and personal with an extraordinarily lifelike "animatronic" dinosaur at the Triceratops Encounter; and prepare to ride the Jurassic Park River Adventure past a further collection of cunningly constructed prehistoric creatures with a dramatic 85-ft (26-m) waterfall plunge as a finale.

The Lost Continent®

A mythical world lost in the mists of time, the Lost Continent draws its inspiration from tales of Greek gods, Arthurian legend and the Arabian Nights. Dominating the skyline is Dueling Dragons®, an intricately designed twin roller-coaster featuring a convincing near-miss scenario; young children are relegated to the scaled-down Flying Unicorn coaster nearby. There are action-packed thrills, stunts and towering pyrotechnic effects involved in The Eighth Voyage of Sindbad® show, but the most elaborate attraction here is Poseidon's Fury® entered via a swirling water vortex hurling 17,500gal (79,545L) of water around a 42-ft (13-m) tunnel. The subsequent battle between the water god and his archrival, Zeus, employs a further 35,000gal (159,091L) of water and flame effects.

Marvel Super Hero Island

Universal's 21st-century technology has been used to create three state-of-the-art thrill rides in this primary-colored, larger-than-life land fit for super heroes. Overhead, the giant green Incredible Hulk Coaster® (it glows in the dark) blasts riders from 0 to 40 mph (65kph) in two seconds before embarking on a heartline inversion, seven roll-overs and two subterranean plunges. Across the street, guests are shot to the top of

the twin 200-ft (61-m) steel towers of Doctor Doom's Fearfall®
before plummeting back down to earth. There is plenty of techno
wizardry on display at the do-not-miss Amazing Adventures of
Spider-Man®, which combines moving ride vehicles, spooky 3-D
action and special effects in a running battle with the forces of evil
out to kidnap the Statue of Liberty; and there is more special
effects action in the Storm Force Accelatron® thrill ride.

Seuss Landing™

From optimum thrills to the whimsical world of Dr. Seuss, this
island is especially geared towards smaller children. An assortment
of suitably bizarre Seussian creatures serve as mounts on the
Caro-Seuss-el, reputed to be the most elaborate carousel ever
built. The One Fish Two Fish Red Fish Blue Fish ride invites guests
to steer their own guppy through a series of water features guided
by a special rhyme: lose the rhyme and get doused by a squirt
post. If I Ran The Zoo is an interactive play area; while the best ride
for accompanying adults is The Cat In The Hat™, an entertaining
journey through scenes from the classic story enlivened by special
effects. Or soar gently above the rides on the High in the Sky
Seuss Trolley Train Ride™.

Toon Lagoon

Betty Boop, Beetle Bailey and Hagar the Horrible leap out of two-dimensions and into outsize "life" on Comic Strip Lane, the main drag of Toon Lagoon. The lagoon in question is home to Me Ship, The Olive, a child-friendly play area aboard Popeye the Sailor's galleon. A short stroll away, Popeye & Bluto's Bilge-Rat Barges® shoot the rapids in a whitewater raft ride that offers an ideal way to cool down on a hot day. And for a distinctly splashy flume ride, the first ever to send passengers below water level, sit tight for Dudley Do-Right's Ripsaw Falls®.

See ► 69 for practical information regarding Universal's Islands of Adventure®.

WET 'N WILD

Best places to see, ► 42–43.

Around Orlando

An all-but-invisible line divides Greater Orlando from neighboring Kissimmee. Walt Disney World® has transformed the former cattle town, bringing a welter of budget hotels and low-priced attractions along US192. Kissimmee is no beauty, but it is a useful family resort area, where the prices are fair, there are thousands of accommodation options and the entertainment is on tap.

Beyond Orlando and Kissimmee, Central Florida offers a wide

choice of attractive day trips. Fast highways lead to top sightseeing destinations such as the Kennedy Space Center on the Atlantic coast and Tampa's Busch Gardens. Equally accessible are the horticultural highlights of Cypress Gardens and Bok Tower Gardens, and there are unspoilt state park preserves where hiking trails, canoe runs and wildlife-spotting provide the perfect antidote to the hurly-burly of the theme parks.

BUSCH GARDENS

A popular side trip from Orlando, Busch Gardens provides a full
day's family entertainment in a sprawling, African-inspired zoo-
cum-theme park complex. The 10 themed areas each offer a choice
of attractions and represents the perfect blend of animal shows,
thrill rides and quiet nature walks. The fun water rides are very
wet, and rainproof capes are on sale, but few sunbaked visitors
bother. However, it is a good idea to bring a change of clothes to
avoid a soggy journey back home. Opposite the Busch Gardens
complex, Anheuser-Busch also have a popular 36-acre (15-ha)
water park, Adventure Island (summer only).
Below is a list of highlights; see also ➤ 28–29.

Bird Gardens

Flamingos, ducks, ibis and koi fish do battle with screeching gulls
for titbits in the leafy lagoon areas of the Bird Gardens. There is a
walk-through aviary, an eagle exhibit, bird shows and captive koala
bears. On the edge of Bird Gardens, the duelling Gwazi roller-
coaster rumbles over its 7,000ft (2,134m) of wooden track.

Congo

An action-packed area at the northern extent of the park, the Congo's attractions include the hair-raising Kumba roller coaster. The slightly less dramatic Python still manages two 360° loops and a 70-ft (21-m) plunge. A drenching is guaranteed on the Congo River Rapids, and onlookers can man the Waterblasters on the bridge (25c a shot). The Ubanga-Banga Bumper Cars are located here, too; the Serengeti Express Railroad train stops at the station; and the park's magnificent Bengal tigers are incarcerated on undersized Claw Island.

Crown Colony

Here you can eat at the park's only full-service dining room, the British Colonial-themed Crown Colony Restaurant. Look in on the Anheuser-Busch brewery's ceremonial draft horses and overlook the expansive Serengeti Plain as you dine on tasty entrees. With everything from salads and sandwiches to fresh seafood platters and filet mignon, the restaurant boasts good food and the air-conditioned environment means a break from the heat.

Egypt

Ruined columns, giant carved figures and hieroglyphics provide the setting for a journey into Tut's Tomb, a walk-through tour of a replica pyramid tomb as discovered by the archaeologist Howard Carter in the 1920s. The contemporary news reel footage is fun, but the jewels look a little pasty. The big ride here is the 3,983-ft (2,214-m) long, 150-ft (46-m) high Montu roller coaster, featuring a heart-stopping inverted loop of 104ft (32m). The Serengeti Express Railroad train travels across the Serengeti Plain.

Land of the Dragons

A well-designed adventure playground for small children, with a friendly dragon theme. The three-story Dragon's Nest treehouse is lavishly equipped with stairs and ropeways, and there are slides, a sandpit, a carousel, watery activities and a children's theater. The Living Dragons display features monitor lizards, Komodo dragons from Indonesia and giant iguanas.

Morocco

At the entrance to the park, Morocco features attractive Moorish-style architecture and a clutch of souk-like stores selling North African craft items. Ice shows are held at the Moroccan Palace Theater and other diversions scheduled in the Marrakesh Theater.

Nairobi

First stop is Myombe Reserve: The Great Ape Domain, where the park's western lowland gorillas and chimpanzees nit-pick, snooze and occasionally stir themselves to get a better look at the humans. There are vampire bats, reptiles and snakes in Curiosity Caverns; baby birds and other residents in the Animal Nursery; a petting zoo, giant tortoises and elephants.

Serengeti Plain

A 60-acre (24-ha) grassland enclosure reminiscent of the African veldt, inhabited by antelopes, giraffes, lions, rhinos and zebras. The park's Edge of Africa adventure promises a safari experience with close-up views of the animals, via a series of imaginatively designed enclosures, complete with a backing track of animal sounds and a range of evocative African smells running the olfactory gamut from camp fire to termite mound. Serengeti also boasts Rhino Rally, a rugged Land Rover Safari experience which packs thrills, spills and over 100 exotic African animals into its 8-minute journey.

Stanleyville

Just the place to cool off with two great water rides: Tanganyika Tidal Wave (which soaks onlookers as well as passengers); and Stanley Falls Log Flume. The new SheiKra roller coaster is the tallest in Florida at 200 feet (61m). There are reptile encounters at Snakes and More; the warthog and orangutan habitats; and a black spider monkey colony cavorting behind the fragrant and colorful Orchid Canyon. Guests can shop for African crafts or enjoy family entertainments at the Stanleyville Theater.

Timbuktu

At the heart of the park, Timbuktu's diversions include a semi-scary 3-D film at R. L. Stine's Haunted Lighthouse; all-singing, all-dancing perfomances at the Desert Grill; thrills aboard the Scorpion roller coaster and other fairground attractions, plus arcade games.

www.buschgardens.com

🚩 134 E1 (off map) ✉ Busch Boulevard, Tampa (75 miles/121km west of
Orlando via I-4 West and I-75 North to Fowler Avenue/Exit 54) ☎ 813/987-
5082 or 1-888 800 5447 🕔 Daily 10–6 (extended summer and hols)
🍴 Refreshment stops throughout park, plus: Zagora Café (Morocco); The
Oasis and Desert Grill (Timbuktu); Crown Colony Restaurant (Crown Colony);
Vivi Storehouse Restaurant (Congo); Zambia Smokehouse (Stanleyville);
Hospitality House (Bird Gardens) ($–$$) 🖐 Very expensive. Orlando
FlexTickets offer reduced rates. Available from participating parks, 5-Park
tickets provide unlimited admission to Busch Gardens, as well as SeaWorld
Orlando, both parks at Universal and Wet 'n Wild over 14 consecutive days.
The park also offers behind-the-scenes tours for an additional charge. A
guide leads groups of up to 15 people on 4–5 hour Guided Adventure Tours;
30-minute Serengeti safaris allow closer contact with the animals; and
groups of 7–10 participate in feeding and training encounters on Animal
Adventure Tours

Serengeti Plain transport

🚃 Crown Colony. Sky Ride cable car: Crown Colony, Stanleyville. Serengeti
Express Railroad: Egypt, Congo, Stanleyville

a drive

A tour around Blue Spring State Park

One of the prettiest state parks in Central Florida, Blue Spring is also famous for its winter season manatee population. They usually visit between November and March, but the park is a great day out all year round, offering walking, boating and swimming opportunites, and it is a good place to enjoy a picnic.

From Orlando, take I-4 east (direction Daytona) to Exit 114. Follow US17-92 2.5 miles (4km) south to Orange City. Blue Spring State Park is signposted off to the right at the junction with W French Avenue.

Lying along the wooded banks of the St. Johns River,
Florida's longest natural waterway, the park's namesake
artesian spring is one of the largest in the US, producing
around 100 million gal (22 million L) of water a day. It really
is blue, too. The turquoise pool at the spring head is a
popular swimming hole for snorkeling, scuba-diving or just
splashing around to cool off in the heat of the day.

During winter the warm spring waters, which gush forth
at a constant 72°F/22°C, attract manatees from the cooler
waters of the St. Johns. From the waterside boardwalk
there is a bird's-eye view of the manatees, and dozens of
different fish and turtles swimming in the spring run;
numerous waterbirds also congregate here. Canoes are
available for rental and there are boat trips down the St.
Johns to nearby Hontoon Island State Park.

*Follow the walking trail that starts near the
Steamboat-era Thursby House.*

Thursby House itself is perched on top of an ancient shell
mound, left by Timucuan Indians. The trail leads through
sand pine scrub, marshland and flatwood areas of the park.

*Return to Orange City and take US17-92/I–4 back to
Orlando.*

Distance 60-mile (97-km) round trip
Time A 45-minute drive from Orlando. Allow at least 2 hours in
the park
Start/end point Orlando
Destination Blue Spring State Park ✉ 2100 W French Avenue,
Orange City ☎ 386/775-3663 ⏰ Daily 8am–sunset 🎫 Inexpensive
Lunch Snack concessions and cold drinks available in the park

CENTRAL FLORIDA ZOOLOGICAL PARK

In a way, the setting of the area's largest zoo distinguishes it from others – it seems to be carved out from the Florida wilderness. You'll exit the interstate highway to reach the zoo, where shaded, winding boardwalks and paths take you from exhibit to exhibit. The usual retinue of animals are here pacing, hanging, strutting, and sleeping in what you wish were larger or more natural enclosures. There are elephants, cheetahs, mandrills and kookaburras and, in the Herpetarium, an impressive line-up of venomous and non-venomous snakes, lizards and frogs. Elsewhere, you'll encounter pumas, llamas, sloths, monkeys, crocodiles and alligators, turtles, iguanas and the beautiful bald eagle. The zoo is about 20 miles (32km) northeast of downtown Orlando in the city of Sanford.

www.centralfloridazoo.org

➕ 134 A4 ✉ US17–92 (south of 1–4/Exit104 toward Sanford) ☎ 407/323-4450 🕐 Daily 9–5, except Thanksgiving and Christmas ✋ Moderate

CONGO RIVER GOLF & EXPLORATION CO

There is a choice of routes around this nifty mini-golf course and players are challenged to follow in the footsteps of 19th-century African explorers Henry Stanley and Dr. David Livingstone. The obstacles are somewhat less dramatic and debilitating than those encountered by our heroes, but the tropical layout is well provided with waterfalls, streams and mountainous boulders beneath the swaying palm trees. For those "too pooped to putt," there are paddle boats and a games arcade. At the second location on International Drive, go-karts add to the fun.

www.congoriver.com

➕ 134 D4 ✉ 4777 W Irlo Bronson Highway/US192 (GM 12), Kissimmee; also at 6312 International Drive, Orlando ☎ 407/396-6900 🕐 Daily 10am–midnight ✋ Moderate

CROSS CREEK

This pleasant quiet rural community is home to the **Majorie Kinnan Rawlings Historic State Park** and well worth a visit if traveling brings you some 60 miles (97km) to the north of Orlando. The author Majorie Kinnan Rawlings lived and worked in the tiny community for two years in the 1930s, where she bought a small homestead and settled down to learn about backwoods Cracker life. She immersed herself in the countryside, learning about every plant, shrub, tree and flower. She cooked on a wood-burning stove and washed her clothes in an iron pot. Neighbours soon warmed to her friendliness and her books reflect an intimate insight into the people and the locality. Her most famous novella was *The Yearling,* for which she won a Pulitzer Prize.

You can visit the house, preserved just as she left it, complete with ancient typewriter on the porch.

✚ 134 A1 (off map)

Marjorie Kinnan Rawlings Historic State Park

✉ Cross Creek (21 miles/34km southeast of Gainesville on CR 325)

☎ 352/466-3672 🕐 Daily 9–5; tours Thu–Sun at 10, 11, 1, 2, 3, 4

✋ Inexpensive

CYPRESS GARDENS ADVENTURE PARK

Best places to see, ➤ 30–31.

FANTASY OF FLIGHT

Vintage planes, each with a story to tell, help illustrate aviation history at this Central Florida aviation attraction. The first thing to notice at Fantasy of Flight is the elegant 1930s and 1940s-style art deco themed buildings, designed to capture the spirit of aviation's Golden Era. Within the twin hangars and parked out on the runways are more than 40 vintage aircraft, just a part of the world's largest private collection built up over the last quarter century by aviation enthusiast Kermit Weeks.

The earliest authentic aircraft on display here, including a

Sopwith Camel, date from World War I. However, illustrating the real dawn of flight, there is a reproduction of the Wright Brothers' 1903 Kitty Hawk Flyer, a cat's-cradle of wires and wooden struts, which has actually flown – if only for a few seconds at a time. A prime Golden Era exhibit with a notable history is the 1929 Ford Tri-Motor. It flew across the US coast-to-coast in 48 hours and was later used in the making of *Indiana Jones and the Temple of Doom*.

The collection of World War II fighter planes from the US, Britain and Germany are among the museum's most popular exhibits, and visitors can test out their air combat skills in the Fightertown Flight Simulators. Another themed "immersion experience" is the History of Flight, which features walk-through dioramas. Backlot Tours take visitors behind the scenes to see the restoration workshops (weather permitting).

www.fantasyofflight.com

✚ 134 E1 ✉ SR559, Polk City (I-4 West to Exit 44) ☎ 863/984-3500
🕐 Daily 10–5 🖐 Expensive 🍴 Compass Rose ($–$$) ❓ Call for details of hot air balloon and biplane rides

GREEN MEADOWS PETTING FARM

A great treat for small children, who can find the theme park experience and crowds a bit overwhelming. Here they can scamper about safely, clamber on tractors, collect acorns for the pigs and encounter other farmyard animals on the two-hour tours. Every child can milk a cow and enjoy waggon and pony rides.

Free-ranging guineafowl, peacocks and chickens peck and preen around the attractive tree-shaded compound, which provides good protection from the hot sun, and toddlers or babies can be towed around in miniature farm trailers. Picnickers are welcome.

www.greenmeadowsfarm.com

🔢 134 D3 ✉ 1368 S Poinciana Boulevard, Kissimmee
☎ 407/846-0770 🕐 Daily 9:30–4 (last tour) 🍴 Snacks, sandwiches and cold drinks available ($) 💰 Expensive

HISTORIC BOK SANCTUARY

Dutch philanthropist and publisher Edward W. Bok created these lovely woodland gardens in the 1920s and added the coquina rock and pink and gray marble bell tower, with its world-class carillon. Its 57 bronze bells range in weight from 17 to more than 22,000 lb (10,000kg) and toll each half hour. The tower is perched on top of Iron Mountain, the highest point on the Florida peninsula, and the gently sloping 157-acre (64-ha) gardens contain thousands of flowering azaleas, camellias and magnolias beneath a canopy of trees. There are tours of the elegant 1930s house and gardens in the grounds on certain days.

www.boksanctuary.org

🔢 134 F3 ✉ CR17-A (off Alt. 27, 3 miles north of Lake Wales)
☎ 863/676-1408 🕐 Daily 8–6 (last admission 5) 💰 Moderate
🍴 Garden Restaurant ($) ❓ Daily carillon recitals at 1 and 3pm; concerts for special events

KENNEDY SPACE CENTER
Best places to see,
➤ 36–37.

KISSIMMEE
Kissimmee is an attractive location for budget travelers. This is the place to find reasonably priced accommodations close to Walt Disney World® Resort, and most hotels offer a free shuttle to the Disney parks. Inexpensive family restaurants are the order of the day along US192, and there are supermarkets for self-catering holidaymakers and plenty of family attractions close by. To help visitors find their way around US192, the city has erected a number of Guide-Markers (GM) along the highway. These are used in this guide to locate the various attractions.

Kissimmee's main road stretches for miles along the US192 east–west cross route, either side of I-4. Its seamless run of local attractions and small shopping centers, chain restaurants and low-rise hotels has been nicely landscaped and made more visitor-friendly with sidewalks and pedestrian access, transportation links and even bicycle racks. The downtown district, at the junction with Orange Blossom Trail, has also been restored.

A recreated turn-of-the-century Main Street, the **Old Town Kissimmee** open-air mall, provides an entertaining mixture of shops and 18 fairground rides, including the landmark Ferris wheel. On Fridays and Saturdays a classic car parade takes place here in the evening.

One of the top rodeo events on the professional Rodeo Cowboys Association southeastern circuit, the **Silver Spurs Rodeo,** takes place at Kissimmee in February and October. It features wild bucking broncos and bulls, calf roping, steer wrestling, barrel racing, rodeo clowns and more.

➕ 134 D4

Old Town Kissimmee

✉ 5770 W Irlo Bronson Memorial Highway/US192 (GM 9), Kissimmee
☎ 407/396-4888 or 1-800 843 4202; www.old-town.com ⏰ 10am–11pm
✋ Free 🍴 Fast food, snacks stalls and several restaurants ($–$$)

Silver Spurs Rodeo

☎ For information call 407/677-6336; www.silverspursrodeo.com

LAKE TOHOPEKALIGA

A short step from downtown Kissimmee, Lake Toho (as it is commonly known) offers an idyllic escape from the crowds. The 13-mile (21-km) long lake covers around 22,700 acres (9,190ha), with several islands in the middle where Seminole Indians once built forts. The bass fishing is excellent, and there is great birdwatching, with more than 120 species of birds living around the lake or visiting – like the winter population of white freshwater pelicans, who fly 2,000 miles (3,225km) south to escape the chilly northern temperatures.

The 30-ft (9-m) Eagle Ray excursion boat takes passengers out on the lake from Big Toho Marina. A number of outfitters offer fishing trips with a knowledgeable guide. There are also several companies offering airboat tours, such as Boggy Creek Airboat & Wildlife Safari Rides.

✚ 134 E4

LAKE WALES

If you'd like to experience Florida before amusement parks cropped up, visit Lake Wales. In a quiet section in the center of the state, there are still groves of oranges, grapefruit and tangerines, plus pristine lakes and Arts and Crafts cottages – and a palpable feeling of old Florida.

The **Lake Wales Museum and Cultural Center,** housed in a former railroad depot on the main street, features local history displays and railroad memorabilia. The other local attraction is Spook Hill, more correctly known as North Wales Drive. Visitors who drive to the bottom of the hill and put their vehicle in neutral at the white line will find that they appear to roll uphill.

✚ 134 F3

Lake Wales Museum and Cultural Center
✉ 325 S Scenic Highway (Alt 27), Lake Wales ☎ 863/678-4209 🕐 Mon–Fri 9–5, Sat 10–4 💰 Inexpensive

REPTILE WORLD SERPENTARIUM

Rather off the beaten track, east of St. Cloud, this no-frills serpentarium's main mission is research, and the collection and distribution of snake venoms. There are cobra and viper venom-gathering programs twice a day (at 12 and 3), and meticulous notes cover each snake display. Discover the secrets of the rattlesnake's tail, learn how to distinguish the non-venomous scarlet king snake from the poisonous eastern coral snake (same black, red and yellow coloring in subtly different proportions), and contemplate the world's largest snake species, the reticulated python and the massive green anaconda, known to snack on crocodiles in its native South America.

✚ 135 D5 ✉ 5705 E Irlo Bronson Memorial Highway/US192, 4 miles (6.5) east of St. Cloud ☎ 407/892-6905 🕓 Tue–Sun 9–5:30. Closed Mon, Thanksgiving and Christmas 🖐 Inexpensive

SILVER SPRINGS

Best places to see, ➤ 40–41.

SPRINGS, CENTRAL FLORIDA

One of the pure pleasures of Central Florida is lazing in the clear, cool waters of its natural springs. This is one of the few places in America where you can do this since a high limestone cap traps crystal clear 72°F (22°C) water just below the surface. The springs – most of which are safely protected within the boundaries of state parks – are just right for swimming, splashing, sunning, and paddling. In DeLand, there's great swimming and cuddly manatees at Blue Springs (➤ 82–83), and a few miles north at DeLeon Springs are the ruins of an old sugar mill and a great swimming hole. In addition to Longwood's Wekiwa Springs, Alexander

Springs and Salt Springs in the Ocala National Forest are two more tranquil swimming pools and each is surrounded by great hiking trails and woodlands. Information on admission prices, directions, and hours are posted on their website.

www.dep.state.fl.us/parks

US ASTRONAUT HALL OF FAME

Now amalgamated with the neighboring Kennedy Space Center, this is a popular stop with children, who enjoy the hands-on approach. There's lots of interactive fun here, along with space hardware exhibits from the Mercury and Gemini programs and entertaining rides such as Shuttle to Tomorrow, a flight into the future aboard a full-scale mock-up of a 120-ft (37-m) orbiter. Potential astronauts get to put themselves to the test with the G-Force Trainer, and another favorite attraction is the stomach-churning 3-D–360° flight simulator ride – which is pretty good fun to watch as well. Many of the exhibits and objects were donated by the astronauts from their personal collections.

✚ 135 C7 ✉ 6225 Vectorspace Boulevard/SR405, Titusville ☎ 321/269-6100
🕐 Daily 9–5 (extended summer and hols) 🖐 Moderate 🍴 Cosmic Cafe ($)

WILD WATERS

This waterpark is the place to cool off on hot summer days after visiting Silver Springs (➤ 40–41) next door. Relax under shady palms and giant oak trees or on the man-made beach. The huge, fan-shaped wave pool is surrounded by lounge chairs and sun decks. For thrill-seekers there are water slides and flume rides, including the Silver Bullet racing flume and the turbo-charged wild water Hurricane.

www.wildwaterspark.com

✚ 134 A1 (off map) ✉ SR40, 1 mile (1.6km) east of Ocala (72 miles/116km northwest of Orlando) ☎ 352/236-2121 🕐 Apr–May and mid-Aug to Sep weekends 10–5, Jun to mid-Aug daily 10–6 🖐 Expensive

WINTER PARK

A smart northern suburb of Orlando, Winter Park boasts a brace of fine art museums, an attractive shopping district and scenic boat trips on a chain of small lakes edged by millionaires' mansions. The town was originally laid out as a genteel winter resort for wealthy New Englanders in the 1880s. Its main street, Park Avenue, is lined with boutiques and art galleries, shops selling exclusive interior design knick-knacks and chic restaurants. On Saturdays, the local Farmers' Market, on New England Avenue, is a favorite stop for fresh produce or for browsing among the colorful stalls.

✚ 134 B4

Morse Museum of American Art

Pride of place goes to the gallery's world-famous collection of Tiffany glass, much of it salvaged from Laurelton Hall, Louis Comfort Tiffany's Long Island home, which burned down in 1957.

Many of Tiffany's own favorite pieces are on display, such as the glorious Rose Window. There are earthy fruit and vegetable stained-glass still lifes, others depicting magnolia blooms and elegant wisteria lampshades.

Further collections cover ceramics, furniture and metalwork, and Tiffany's contemporaries also get a look in, with glassware from René Lalique and

Emile Galle, paintings by Maxfield Parrish, and contributions from
Frank Lloyd Wright.

✉ 445 Park Avenue, Winter Park ☎ 407/645-5311; www.morsemuseum.org
🕐 Tue–Sat 9:30–4, Sun 1–4. Closed Mon and major hols ✋ Inexpensive

Rollins College and Cornell Fine Arts Museum

At the southern end of Park Avenue is the delightful campus of
Florida's oldest college. Established in 1885, Rollins' original
campus buildings were constructed in fashionable Spanish-
Mediterranean style on a pretty campus overlooking Lake Virginia.
Near the entrance to the campus, the Walk of Fame features more
than 400 stepping stones gathered from the birthplaces and
homes of famous people, from Mary, Queen of Scots and
Benjamin Franklin to Buffalo Bill. There is an attractive college
chapel and theater linked by a loggia, and the Cornell Fine Arts
Museum houses notable collections of European Old Master
paintings, 19th- and 20th-century American art, Indian objects and
decorative arts.

✉ Rollins College, Holt Avenue, Winter Park ☎ 407/646-2526;
www.rollins.edu/cfam 🕐 Cornell Fine Arts Museum: Tue–Sat 10–5, Sun 1–5.
Closed Mon ✋ Inexpensive

Scenic Boat Tours

A chain of six little freshwater lakes around Winter Park is linked by
narrow, leafy canals. The canals were once used to transport logs,
but now facilitate the movement of small boats and allow scenic
boat trips to putter from Lake Osceola down to Lake Virginia and
up to Lake Maitland. The tours last about an hour and offer a prime
view of Winter Park's most exclusive lake frontage – the grandest
homes overlook Lake Maitland. Waterbirds are easy to spot and
there is the occasional glimpse of an alligator.

✉ 312 E Morse Boulevard, Winter Park ☎ 407/644-4056;
www.scenicboattours.com 🕐 Daily 10–4 on the hour, except Christmas
✋ Moderate

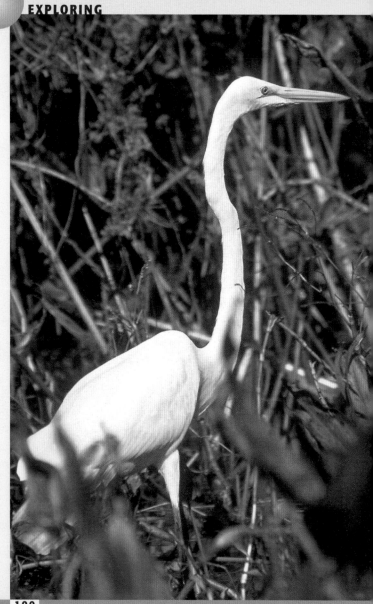

Walt Disney World® Resort

**Walt Disney World® Resort
is the apogee of the Disney
phenomenon. It is a
fairytale fiefdom, where
litter and spoilsports are
banned and Cinderella
Castle pops out of the
storybook and into 3-D
reality. Disney's appeal is
universal. It makes nonsense of age
and cultural barriers uniting people from all walks
of life in the pursuit of good, clean family fun and
escapist fantasy. Teams of "imagineers" have
resurrected everybody's favorite characters, then
added the latest
screen stars, state-of-
the-art rides, shows
and even gently
educational exhibits
spread over the theme
parks, water parks and
entertainment
districts.**

Some find it all too perfect,
and Disney's reputation for
ruthless efficiency leads to
charges of blandness.
However, the prime
objective here is family
entertainment and that,
even the most grudging
cynic has to admit, Disney
delivers in abundance.

© Disney

VISITING WALT DISNEY WORLD® RESORT

The cooler winter months are the most comfortable time to visit Walt Disney World® Resort, and the crowds are definitely less pressing either side of the Christmas rush (January until mid-February, and mid-September until Christmas, with the exception of the busy Thanksgiving holiday). However, expect to stand in line whenever you go, and be well prepared with loose, comfy clothing, sturdy footwear and sunblock.

Ticket options: Daily One Park/One Day admission tickets are valid for one park only on the stated day but if you plan to stay for several days, which you should do, multiple-day "Magic Your Way" base tickets offer flexibility and savings. The multi-day passes are good for one park each day your ticket is valid. For an additional

© Disney

$35, you can add the "park hopper" option to a ticket and have the privilege of racing from one park to the next. Another add-on is the Magic Plus Pack, which will cover admission to Disney's water parks, Pleasure Island, or the DisneyQuest® video arcade. It is best to do your homework before you arrive and check online for ticket configurations. Keep in mind that unless you purchase the additional "no expiration" option, tickets now expire 14 days after their first day of use. Guests at certain properties can purchase the **Ultimate Park Hopper,** which provides admission to all Disney's WDW attractions.

FASTPASS®: Save time standing in line for the most popular rides in all four Disney theme parks with the FASTPASS® system. Simply pop your regular park ticket into the FASTPASS® machine at the attractions offering the complimentary service and you will receive a designated return time with no need to wait. The FASTPASS® allows a one-hour window from the time printed on the ticket during which you should present yourself at the FASTPASS® entrance with your ticket and sail straight through. You can only have one FASTPASS® running at any one time, i.e. you must have used (or exceeded the time allocation for) one FASTPASS® before you can collect another. Attractions offering this service are indicated on Disney maps and in this guide by the letters (FP).

What to expect: The Disney parks provide a wide range of guest facilities, from baby strollers and lockers to banking and kenneling. A limited number of wheelchairs are available, and there are special arrangements for sight- and hearing-impaired visitors. Guest relations can also help with lost and found queries, camera rentals and free battery-charging.

http://disneyworld.disney.go.com

✚ 140 D4 ✉ Walt Disney World® Resort, Lake Buena Vista (I-4/several exits and US 192, south of Orlando) ☎ 407/824-4321 ◉ Check current schedules ✋ Very expensive. Note that children of 10 and over qualify for adult tickets; children's tickets are for ages 3–9; under 3 free ⬛ Each park offers a wide choice of dining options open throughout the day. Reservations are advised for table service restaurants (☎ 407/939-3463) 🚌 Free shuttle bus services from many Orlando/Kissimmee hotels ❓ Details of daily parades, showtimes and night-time displays are printed in current park guides. Hotel, campground, show and ticket reservations can be made through Central Reservations (☎ 407/934-7639). Dining reservations can be made up to 60 days in advance or 180 days if you're staying at a Disney resort (☎ 407/939-3463)

© Disney

BLIZZARD BEACH

Water sports are the specialty of Blizzard Beach, a northern ski-resort-gone-tropical water park, where the chair lifts sport sun umbrellas and the slalom course is a waterslide.

The 60-acre (24-ha) site boasts a dozen different adventure zones in the shadow of "snow-covered" Mount Gushmore. Take a chair lift up to the 60mph (97kph) Summit Plummet slide, or the slightly less dramatic Slush Gusher. Other top attractions include the Teamboat Springs white-water raft ride, inner tubing down Runoff Rapids, and the Snow Stormers flumes.

On a less frenetic note, lazy Cross Country Creek circles the park and a sandy beach borders the wave pool below Mount Gushmore. Little children can play safely at Tike's Peak; and there is shopping for essentials and souvenirs in The Village.

✚ 140 F3 ✉ W Buena Vista Drive, Walt Disney World® Resort ☎ 407/939-7529 🕐 Daily 10–5 (extended summer and hols) 💷 Expensive (or available as option with Park Hopper Plus Pass) 🍴 Lottawatta Lodge ($–$$), Avalunch and The Warming Hut snack bars ($)

DISNEY'S ANIMAL KINGDOM® PARK

Walt Disney World® Resort's fourth full-scale theme park, Disney's Animal Kingdom® Park, focuses Disney's imagination on the natural world. The 500-acre (202-ha) site features five themed districts and has more than 200 animal species showcased in re-created naturalistic habitats. Not content with the wonders of the world about us, Disney has also gone for a fun celebration of the dinosaur era with DinoLand U.S.A®. Among all the fun, however, care has been taken to incorporate a conservationist message.

For the best chance of seeing the animals at their most active, it pays off to arrive at Disney's Animal Kingdom® as early as possible. From The Oasis entry point, head for Discovery Island® and the footbridge links to the other four districts. Then secure your first FASTPASS® (▶ 103) and check schedules for Mickey's Jammin' Jungle Parade, which tootles through the kingdom.

Africa

African-styled Harambe Village is the start point for
two excellent big game viewing opportunities.
Kilimanjaro Safaris (FP) is one ride not to be missed
in Disney's Animal Kingdom®, a Jeep journey deep
into the re-created African veldt inhabited by lions,
cheetahs, rhinos, giraffes, wildebeest, zebras and
others. The ride is brought to a rather abrupt end by a
rescue mission to save the elephants from poachers,
but the Pangani Forest Exploration Trail allows a
closer look at some of the safari animals, notably an
underwater view of the hippos, plus a lush and misty
gorilla habitat. Mosey on down to Harambe Station
to catch the Wildlife Express miniature train ride,
which wends its way past the "backlot" animal
quarters to Rafiki's Planet Watch. Here exhibits on
endangered species are presented alongside picture
windows viewing into the animal nursery and
veterinary suite.

Asia

Exuberant rainforest-type foliage and colorful tropical
flowers set the tone for the Maharaja Jungle Trek, a
gentle stroll through elaborate Indian temple ruins to
the tiger enclosure and exotic bird aviaries. After the
trek, visit the Flights of Wonder birds of prey show,
or down a cool drink in the leafy Siamang Viewing
Area. Asia's action adventure is the Kali River Rapids
(FP), a whitewater rafting ride that shoots beneath
tunnels of overhanging bamboo, past giant boulders
and cooling water jets. A new roller coaster ride,
Expedition Everest, creates cutting edge excitement
as it rushes forwards, backwards, up and down as
you try to steer clear of the Abominable Snowman.

© Disney

Camp Minnie-Mickey

Set slightly away from the main bustle, this is a good place for families with young children to take a break. Camp Minnie-Mickey's character greeting areas field a full team of classic Disney figures. Pocahontas and Her Forest Friends is a cute child-oriented show with live animal performers; while the Festival of the Lion King is a real crowd-pleasing spectacular for all ages, featuring acrobatic routines, fire-jugglers and stilt-walkers.

DinoLand U.S.A.®

Prehistory with a Disneyesque spin begins at the Olden Gate Bridge, a 40-ft (12-m) Brachiosaurus skeleton marking the entrance to DinoLand U.S.A®. First stop for kids is The Boneyard play area. Follow this with a visit to the Fossil Preparation Lab, where real life paleontologists undertake their research into dinosaur remains, while guests are dwarfed by the impressive collection of life-size

© Disney

casts taken from dinosaur skeletons in the Dinosaur Jubilee exhibition area. On the thrills front, there is rollercoaster action aboard Primeval Whirl! and the Dinosaur (FP) ride is a must, offering a time travel expedition back to the end of the dinosaur era. Dodge meteorite showers and ravening, blood-thirsty "animatronic" dinosaurs in an attempt to bring back a dear little veggie dino for posterity. For light relief, check out Finding Nemo – The Musical at the Theater in the Wild or take a four-person dino vehicle for a gentle "dino soar" with TriceraTop Spin.

Discovery Island®

At the heart of Discovery Island®, the Tree of Life is the centerpiece and symbol of the park. The trunk, branches and root system of the 145-ft (44-m) tall landmark have been carved with 325 animal images and around its vast bulk the Discovery Island® Trails meander past assorted enclosures for lemurs,

kangaroos, capybaras and other small- to medium-sized animals. Beneath the roots, a subterranean theater presents It's Tough to be a Bug® (FP), an entertaining 3-D look at life from a bug's perspective starring Flik and Hopper from *A Bug's Life*. (Some effects could upset small children.)
➕ 140 F2 ✉ Osceola Parkway, Walt Disney World® Resort ☎ 407/824-4321 🕐 Check current schedules

DISNEY'S HOLLYWOOD STUDIOS

Disney's Hollywood Studios (formerly Disney-MGM Studios) was Walt Disney World® Resort's riposte to the news that Universal Studios® was opening a rival theme park-cum-studio facility at Orlando in 1990. Disney squeezed in just ahead, opening in 1989, and have almost doubled the size of the original park, though it remains rather shorter on rides than its chief rival. However, there is plenty of Disney flair on display and constantly updated exhibits showcase new productions. Overleaf are some highlights:
➕ 140 F3 ✉ Walt Disney World® Resort ☎ 407/824-4321

Backlot Tour

After a visit to the splash tank hop aboard a tram to cruise past the Star's Parking Lot, the world's largest working wardrobe department, and the props and special effects departments. There are a couple of surprises at Catastrophe Canyon before arriving at the American Film Institute Showcase for a display of prize props and film memorabilia.

The Great Movie Ride

On Hollywood Boulevard a full-scale re-creation of Mann's Chinese Theater is the setting for this ambitious homage to movie classics. Audio-Animatronics® figures replace the stars in famous scenes.

"Honey, I Shrunk the Kids" Movie Set Adventure

An imaginative children's adventure play area featuring giant bugs, looming blades of grass and cooling water jets.

Indiana Jones® Epic Stunt Spectacular! (FP)

Check schedules with the updated show times listed in the park's free map, and catch a performance of this explosive stunt show. "Audience volunteers" get an opportunity to join in the fun.

Muppet Vision 3-D (FP)

Jim Henson's magnificent Muppets steal the show hands down. A terrific combination of big screen 70mm, 3-D film action, monster special effects and anarchic humor.

The Magic of Disney Animation

A brief but illuminating insight into the world of animation. Check out the original artworks in the animation gallery before the tour leads off through the production studios.

Rock 'n' Roller Coaster® Starring Aerosmith (FP)

A giant red electric guitar fronts this thrilling roller-coaster ride in the dark accompanied by a thumping soundtrack and some pretty hairy maneuvres.

Star Tours

A bone-shaking intergalatic thrill ride on a runaway space ship. Wild simulator action and dazzling special effects.

Theater of the Stars

In a setting reminiscent of the Hollywood Bowl, the 1,500-seat Theater of the Stars hosts Beauty and the Beast Live – a cute mini-musical that kids love. The Hollywood Hills Amphitheatre is the setting for Fantasmic! – an evening extravaganza featuring fireworks, action songs and a salute to Disney film and music classics. It is hugely popular so arrive early for a good seat.

The Twilight Zone Tower of Terror™ (FP)

A quiet stroll down Sunset Boulevard is soon interrupted by the shrieks of terrified passengers plummeting down the lift shaft of the spooky Hollywood Tower Hotel. Guests encounter various mysterious manifestations on the route to the top of the 199-ft (61-m) building before a series of plunges. Don't miss it.

Voyage of The Little Mermaid (FP)

Beloved of little girls the world over, Ariel gets the full theme park treatment as her story is retold with clever special effects, puppets, Audio-Animatronics, film clips and live performers.

Walt Disney: One Man's Dream

Compiled as part of Disney's 100 Years of Magic Celebration!, this look at the theme park visionary's life and achievements features objects and previously unseen film footage.

© Disney

DOWNTOWN DISNEY®

On the shores of Lake Buena Vista, the ever-expanding Downtown Disney® shopping, dining and entertainment complex encompasses three distinct districts: the Marketplace; Pleasure Island (➤ 127); and the rapidly expanding West Side attractions area.

Down on the lakeside, the Marketplace combines a selection of colorful boutiques and souvenir shopping outlets with a handful of restaurants, including the landmark Rainforest Café), crowned by a volcano. During the day there are pedalboats for rental from the dock.

The neon-lit West Side boasts the state-of-the-art DisneyQuest® interactive games attraction, a 24-screen cinema complex, Virgin Records Megastore and the Cirque du Soleil®, a 1,650-seat theater that stages glitzy, high-energy acrobatic and modern dance productions. Notable dining and entertainment venues include Orlando outposts of the House of Blues, Planet Hollywood, Wolfgang Puck Café and Gloria Estefan's Bongos Cuban Café.

✚ 141 E5 ✉ E Buena Vista Drive, Walt Disney World® Resort ☎ 407/939-2648 🕐 Daily. Most shops stay open until 11pm or midnight; restaurants until midnight or 2am 👋 Free. Admission charged to DisneyQuest and for concerts and shows ❓ Information and reservations for Cirque du Soleil®, ☎ 407/939-7600; DisneyQuest® 407/828-4600

EPCOT®

Walt Disney's original plan to create a Utopian-style research community living on the Epcot® (Experimental Prototype Community of Tomorrow) site never came to fruition, but his ideas have been adapted to provide a semi-educational showcase for new technology and sciences and a window on the world around us.

Epcot®, twice the size of Magic Kingdom®, and twice as tough to navigate on foot, is divided into two parts. In the shadow of a giant silver geosphere, the **Future World** (► 114–117) pavilions house the scientific stuff, with displays focusing on transport, communications, health, energy, agriculture and oceanology. This sounds rather serious, but the Walt Disney Imagineers have added plenty of hands-on fun, rides and film shows.

The second section of the park is **World Showcase** (► 118–119), a 1.3-mile (2-km) promenade through 11 "villages," each representing the potted history, culture and architecture of a different nation.

🕂 140 E4 ✉ Epcot® Center Drive, Walt Disney World® Resort ☎ 407/824-4321 🕃 Check schedules

Recommended Epcot® Restaurants

🍽 Future World: Coral Reef, The Living Seas World Showcase: Chefs de France, France; L'Originale Alfredo di Roma, Italy; Nine Dragons, China; Mitsukoshi Teppan Yaki Dining Room, Japan

❓ Make lunch or dinner reservations at Guest Relations on entering the park

EPCOT® – FUTURE WORLD
Innoventions

Tomorrow's technology today, as top companies preview the latest developments in science and technology in an interactive environment. The two Innoventions pavilions are packed with hands-on fun from virtual tag games with Mickey and Minnie to video challenges designed to test players' problem-solving skills and knowledge of a range of science, technology and environmental subjects. Guests can build a family homepage at the Web Site Construction Zone, check out the future of the automobile, and tour the "smarthome" of tomorrow, which includes a robot dog amongst its innovations.

Journey into Imagination with Figment

A lackluster presentation narrated by Monty Python stalwart Eric Idle, who shares the billing with a perky little dragon called Figment. The ride grinds through a series of colorful scenes purporting to represent an exploration of human imagination and

© Disney

deposits bemused passengers into the interactive ImageWorks area to experiment with their own images. Much more fun is the hugely entertaining Honey, I Shrunk the Audience (FP) 3-D show in the movie theater.

The Land

There are three deservedly popular attractions here, starting with Living with the Land (FP). This gentle boat ride journeys through various environments explaining how plants survive, then continues into a futuristic greenhouse world where some of the fresh produce served in Walt Disney World® Resort restaurants is grown. This is quite a sight as you glide past citrus trees laden with giant 9-lb (4-kg) lemons (each capable of producing two pints of juice) and string gardens where cucumbers, eggplants and banks of lettuces grow vertically. Guests who would like a closer look at The Land's experimental greenhouses should sign up for Behind The Seeds, a behind-the-scenes guided walk tour.

Near the entrance to The Land, the Circle of Life in the Harvest

© Disney

Theater is an excellent eco-conscious film show starring characters from *The Lion King:* Simba the Lion King turns Simba-the-Educator and talks Pumbaa and Timon out of polluting Africa with the Hakuna Matata Electric Disco Holiday Resort. Pretty hard-hitting stuff for Orlando.

A highly popular ride is Soarin™. Sitting under the wings of a hang glider, you're hoisted 40ft (12m) high inside a giant projection screen dome, then you take off on a virtual aerial tour of California.

The Seas with Nemo and Friends
The former Living Seas pavilion, now revamped with the popular film characters, features a 6-million-gallon salt water marine exhibit with an amazing man-made coral reef inhabited by 2,000 colorful and curious tropical fish. A ride on the clam-mobile takes you into the coral reef with views of sharks, dolphins and sea turtles. Manatees, Florida's endangered prehistoric sea cows, also feature.

Mission: SPACE
A high-tech, high-thrill ride that simulates a space adventure and launches you from a pulse-racing, adrenaline-injected lift-off to a rendezvous with weightlessness and a rough landing on Mars.

Spaceship Earth
A ride through the history of communications within the focal point of the park – a 180-ft (55-m) high aluminum geosphere. Dioramas illustrate man's progress from cave paintings to a neon journey down the Information Superhighway. Then passengers

disembark into the AT&T Global Neighborhood and its diverting assortment of hands-on games with a futuristic flavor.

Test Track (FP)

The longest and fastest ride ever created by Walt Disney Imagineers features road test automobile action. Take to the track for a tyre-squealing, three-story ascent and assorted high-speed maneuvres in the dark.

Universe of Energy

Ellen Degeneres stars with Bill Nye, the Science Guy, in a multi-screen – and occasionally humorous – presentation of the history and uses of energy. A long pre-show is just the beginning. The entire presentation lasts 45 minutes, which is a lot of valuable vacation time spent watching fake dinosaurs and hearing about an oil giant's take on fossil fuels.

© Disney

EPCOT® – WORLD SHOWCASE
The American Adventure
The centerpiece of the World Showcase villages presents a
30-minute dramatized history of America by Audio-Animatronic
American icons Mark Twain and Benjamin Franklin.

Canada
Feast the eyes on the CircleVision 360° *O Canada!* film and stock
up on maple leaf motifs at a Rockies-style exhibit.

China
A beautiful 360° film of Chinese
people and landmarks, museum-
quality displays of historic objects
and fabulously elaborate architecture.

© Disney

France
Re-created belle époque Paris in the
shadow of a miniature Eiffel Tower.
Café dining, wine-tasting, waterfront
artists and a French perfumerie.

Germany
Storybook architecture with geranium-filled window boxes, plus
traditional "oompah" music piped out over the popular *biergarten*.

Italy
Venice's St. Mark's Square and the Doge's Palace recreated with
scaled-down precision, along with ice creams, arias and gondolas.

Japan
Wind chimes, temple drums and a pagoda, set beside manicured
gardens and koi fish ponds, give an authentic twist to this
shopping and dining complex.

© Disney

Mexico
A huge model of a pre-Columbian pyramid and a boat ride down the River of Time attract plenty of visitors.

Morocco
An attractive Moorish souk set in narrow alleys and elegant tiled courtyards. Belly-dancing displays in the restaurant.

Norway
Malevolent trolls summon up a North Sea storm to rock the good ship *Maelstrom* (FP), a Viking longboat thrill ride in this popular Scandinavian village.

United Kingdom
Or, rather, Merrie England: a jolly knees-up with Cockney pearly kings and queens in the Rose & Crown Pub, fish and chips, warm beer and street entertainers massacring Shakespeare.

MAGIC KINGDOM®

The Disney theme park that nobody wants to miss is, as a result, the most crowded, overwhelming and deserving of a second visit if you have time. Dominated by the fulsomely turreted and spired fairytale folly of Cinderella Castle, seven themed lands spread out over the 100-acre (40-ha) site, and there are 40-plus adventure attractions, dozens of daily shows, and Disney characters at every turn.

 140 C2 ⊠ World Drive, Walt Disney World® Resort ☎ 407/824-4321
🕐 Check current schedules

© Disney

Transportation to the Magic Kingdom®

🚌 Shuttle buses pick up and drop off regularly at Transportation and Ticket Center ⛴ Ferry crosses Seven Seas Lagoon into Park; also monorail from Transportation and Ticket Center

Transportation within the Magic Kingdom®

🚆 Walt Disney World® Railroad circles the perimeter of the park, starting at main entrance, with stops at Frontierland and Mickey's Toontown Fair. Tomorrowland® Transit Authority loop ride operates within Tomorrowland®.

Cartoon Characters

✉ Disney Character Greeting Locations, highlighted on free map guides 🍴 Character dining at The Crystal Palace (Main Street); Liberty Tree Tavern (dinner only, Liberty Square); character breakfasts and lunches in Fantasyland at Cinderella's Royal Table (reservations from the City Hall information centre). For schedules and reservations: ☎ 407/939-3463

Shows and Parades

Tribute shows in the Castle Forecourt and Fantasyland several times a day. Daily, all-singing, all-dancing parade on Main Street, USA at 3pm. Check schedules for the SpectroMagic night-time parade and Wishes fireworks (nightly).

Adventureland

Lush tropical plants and eclectic colonial architecture set the scene for some of the adventures in the park. Explore the ingenious Swiss Family Treehouse, laid out amid the branches of a giant (plastic) banyan tree, and grab a pith helmet from the explorers' outfitters for a gentle rainforest Jungle Cruise (FP), which is one of the park's must-see attractions. The fast-talking skippers deliver a series of snappy one-liners on the ten-minute cruise to create an unforgettably fun adventure. Next door, the excellent Pirates of the

© Disney

Caribbean adventure is a rollicking boat journey into pirate territory with noisy special effects, Audio-Animatronics buccaneers, caves full of plundered loot and a marine attack on a Caribbean island. On a less bloodthirsty note, kids will love dodging the waterspewing camels on The Magic Carpets of Aladdin, and singing totem poles and flowers join the original Tiki Birds from Disney's first-ever Audio-Animatronics show for a "hipper" version of The Enchanted Tiki Room – Under New Management.

Fantasyland

Gathered at the foot of Cinderella Castle, rides and shows are based on storybook characters designed to appeal to smaller children. Classic fairground rides include the prancing, gilded horses of Cinderella's Golden Carrousel, the whirlygig cups and saucers of the Mad Tea Party and the two-man pachyderms of Dumbo the Flying Elephant. Children can enjoy The Many Adventures of Winnie the Pooh (FP); cool off playing in the waterspouts at Ariel's Grotto; or float through the excruciatingly cute It's a Small World singing doll exhibit. Mickey's PhilharMagic (FP) is a thoroughly entertaining 3-D film where Donald Duck takes a wild ride through scenes with Aladdin, Ariel (Little Mermaid) and Simba (Lion King); 4-D sensations

© Disney

include splashes of water, gusts of wind and pleasing scents.

Frontierland®

A step back in time to the Old West with stores, a shooting gallery and good thrill rides. The runaway log flume action at Splash Mountain® (FP) kicks up enough of a wave to cool off onlookers, while the Big Thunder Mountain Railroad (FP) takes passengers on a whoopin' and hollerin' roller-coaster ride. Motorized rafts potter across to Tom Sawyer Island.

Liberty Square

A genteel counterpoint to the bedlam of the neighboring Frontierland, Liberty Square has a more East Coast colonial feel and a patriotic spreading live oak, known as the Liberty Tree. Here, the Hall of Presidents presentation tackles American history in a series of lectures delivered by Audio-Animatronics US presidents. More lively by far are the undead in the Haunted Mansion (FP). This schlock-horror attraction through curtains of cobwebs, rattling bones and shrieking holograms is more rib-tickling than scary, but it's worth braving the lines. In addition, there are boat trips on the *Liberty Belle* Riverboat.

Main Street, U.S.A.

A prettified Victorian street scene, said to have been inspired by Walt Disney's childhood home in Marceline, Missouri, this broad avenue leads from the front gate up to Cinderella Castle at the hub of the park. Near the gates, in Town Square, City Hall is the main information center and depot for the horse-drawn carriages and trams that trundle up Main Street to the castle. The square also has tree-shaded areas where regular concerts are held by the Main Street Rythm Rascals. All along the route to the castle, shops sell a variety of Disney merchandise and gifts. If just arriving at the park has whetted your appetite, there's an ice-cream parlor and a bake shop.

Mickey's Toontown Fair

Home to Mickey and Minnie, this colorful corner of the park is a huge favorite with little children. Take a tour around Minnie's Country House – a veritable symphony in lilac and pink hearts and flowers with a garden to match. Mickey's Country House, next door, as you might expect, displays wardrobes full of the signature red trousers, black jackets and big boots and Pluto's dog kennel is in the garden. Children can cool off in the Donald's Boat play area, thoughtfully equipped with a bungee-soft floor and water jets; and there are pint-sized thrills to be had on The Barnstormer at Goofy's Wiseacre Farm roller-coaster.

Tomorrowland®

Dramatically updated and revamped, but top of the list here is still Space Mountain® (FP), a terrific roller-coaster ride in the dark that many rate as the top ride in the park. Tomorrowland® Indy Speedway is enduringly popular, too. Stitch's Great Escape!™ (FP) puts you on the trail of the wild, loveable alien. You join the Galactic Federation to capture Stitch, which is simply a storyline designed to introduce blackouts, weird noises and occasionally scary sensations. Further into Tomorrowland®, there are more interactive thrills aboard Buzz Lightyear's Space Ranger Spin (FP) as riders battle the evil Zurg with lasers.

On a rather gentler note, there's slapstick and belly laughs from the crew at Monsters Inc Laugh Floor. Take flight in the Astro

© Disney

Orbiter, a mini-rocket ship ride that resembles a chunk of 1950s space cartoon hardware, but does afford a good view of the area, as does the Tomorrowland® Transit Authority, which detours into the bowels of Space Mountain® to listen to the roller-coaster passengers' screams. Debuted way back at the 1964 New York World's Fair, Walt Disney's Carousel of Progress has its share of loyal fans, but in truth this stilted Audio-Animatronics nostalgia-fest is unlikely to appeal to anybody under 60.

© Disney

PLEASURE ISLAND

A 6-acre (2.5-ha) nighttime entertainment complex, Pleasure Island's one-off admission ticket entitles guests to party the night away in any or all of its eight nightclubs. There is also shopping, dining, movie theaters and dancing in the streets. Several of the shops are open during the day, when admission is free, but the real action (and paid admission) starts at 7pm and builds to a midnight New Year's Eve Street Party, complete with fireworks and a blizzard of confetti every night of the year. The revelry continues until 2am.

The night clubs run the gamut from The Comedy Warehouse, with its nightly improvisational comedy shows, to the Rock 'n' Roll Beach Club, which serves up live bands and DJs spinning hits from the 1960s up to the present day. Need to unwind after a hectic day? Then check out the music, dance and storytelling at Raglan's Road's Irish Pub. Still got energy to burn? Lava lamps and mirror balls are all the rage at 1970s-style 8 Trax; for more contemporary sounds, hit Motion, Mannequins Dance Palace or the BET Soundstage™ Club for the best in high-energy hip-hop and R&B. For something completely different, sample the interactive comedy and general weirdness on offer at the Adventurers Club.

➕ 141 E5 ✉ E Buena Vista Drive, Walt Disney World® Resort ☎ 407/934-7781 🕐 Daily, shops 10am–1am; clubs 7 or 8pm–2am 🍴 Light dining in the clubs ($$), also access to the Marketplace restaurants 👋 Expensive (or available as option with Park Hopper Plus Pass). Additional charge for movie theaters. Occasional additional charge for special shows in specific clubs ❓ Under 18s must be accompanied by a parent; for admission to BET Soundstage™ Club and Mannequins guests must be 21 or older. All guests need a photo ID such as a passport or driving license to buy alcohol

TYPHOON LAGOON

An impressive water park with an artfully shipwrecked feel, Typhoon Lagoon's showpiece is the 2.5-acre (1-ha) lagoon with surf-sized 6-ft (2-m) waves rolling onto sandy beaches every 90 seconds. Rocky Mount Mayday is landscaped with flumes and waterslides, and snorkelers can explore the 362,000-gal (79,640-L) salt-water coral reef environment, Shark Reef, inhabited by real tropical fish. For the biggest thrills in the park, though, check out Humunga Kowabunga, an awesome trio of 30-mph (48-kph) waterslides. The Crush 'n' Gusher water coaster ride is also highly recommended; and there is the separate Ketchakidee Creek water playground for little children.

🚩 141 E5 ✉ Epcot® Center Drive, Walt Disney World® Resort ☎ 407/824-4321 🕐 Daily 10–5 (extended summer and hols) 🍴 Leaning Palms ($), Typhoon Tilly's ($) 💲 Expensive (or available as option with Park Hopper Plus Pass)

© Disney

Index

Acknowledgements

The Automobile Association wishes to thank the following photographers, companies and picture libraries for their assistance in the preparation of this book.

Abbreviations for the picture credits are as follows – (t) top; (b) bottom; (l) left; (r) right; (c) centre; (AA) AA World Travel Library.

4l News Stands, Orlando, AA/P Bennett; **4c** Big Thunder Mountain, © Disney; **4r** Gatorland, AA/P Bennett; **5l** Winter Park Golf, AA/P Bennett; **5c** Main Street, Old Town, Kissimmee, AA/P Bennett; **6** Hulk Roller Coast, Islands of Adventure, AA/P Bennett; **7** Shamu Killer Whale Show, Sea World, AA/P Bennett; **8/9** City Walk at night, AA/P Bennett; **10** Big Tree Park, AA/P Bennett; **11** Trompe L'Oeil, Universal Studios, AA/P Bennett; **12/13** News Stands, Orlando, AA/P Bennett; **16** Fort Liberty, AA/T Souter; **18/19** Lynx Bus, International Drive, AA/P Bennett; **20t** I-Ride bus, AA/P Bennett; **20b** Yellow taxis, AA/P Bennett; **23** Post Box, AA/C Sawyer; **26/27** Big Thunder Moutnain, © Disney; **28** Pirate Ride Busch Gardens, Busch Gardens; **28/29** Flume Ride, Busch Gardens; **30/31t** Cypress Gardens, AA/T Souter; **30/31b** Cypress Gardens, AA/T Souter; **32** Discovery Cove, Dolphin interaction, AA/P Bennett; **32/33** Wet and Wild, AA/P Bennett; **34/35** Leu Gardens, Leu Gardens; **35** Rose at Leu Gardens, Leu Gardens; **36** Kennedy Space Center, AA/P Bennett; **37** Kennedy Space Center, AA/P Bennett; **38/39t** Whale, Shamu Show, Sea World, AA/P Bennett; **38/39b** Whale, Shamu Show, Sea World, AA/P Bennett; **39** Sea World sign, Orlando, AA/P Bennett; **40/41** Silver Springs National Park, Alamy/David Lyons; **42/43t** Wet n Wild, AA/P Bennett; **42/43b** Wet n Wild, AA/P Bennett; **44** Cinderella Castle, © Disney; **44/45** Cinderella Castle, © Disney; **46/47t** Shrek 4D, Universal Orlando; **46/47b** Entrance to Universal Orlando, Universal Orlando; **48/49** Gatorland, AAP Bennett; **51** Python, Gatorland, AA/P Bennett; **52/53** Alligators, Gatorland, AA/P Bennett; **54/55** Menello Museum, painting by Earl Cunningham, Menello Museum; **56/57t** Children at the Orlando Science Center, Orlando Science Center; **56/57b** Orlando Science Center by night, Orlando Science Center; **58** Ripley's Believe it or Not, AA/T Souter; **58/59** Ripley's Believe it or Not, AA/P Bennett; **60** Dolphin in Seaworld, AA/T Souter; **61** Journey to Atlantis Ride, Sea World, AA/P Bennett; **62/63t** Sealion, Pirate Show, Sea World, AA/P Bennett; **62/63b** Manatee Pool, Seaworld, AA/P Bennett; **64/65** Hollywood Diner, Universal Studios, AA/P Bennett; **66** Hollywood Diner, Universal Studios, AA/P Bennett; **67** Universal Studios, AA/P Bennett; **68/69** Café, Universal Studios, AA/P Bennett; **69** Universal Studios entrance, AA/P Bennett; **70/71** Lost Continents, Islands of Adventure, AA/P Bennett; **71** Islands of Adventure Logo, Universal Studios; **72** Popeye's Galleon, Universal Studios; **72/73** Lost Continents, Island of Adventure, AA/P Bennett; **74** Bok Tower Gardens, AA/P Bennett; **75** Kissimmee, AA/P Bennett; **76/77** Busch Gardens, AA/P Bennett; **78/79** Giraffe, Busch Gardens, AA/P Bennett; **80/81** Ride at Busch Gardens, Busch Gardens; **82** Homosassa Springs State Wildlife Park, AA/P Bennett; **84/85** Python, Central Florida Zoo, AA/P Bennett; **85** Elephant Enclosure, Central Florida Zoo, AA/P Bennett; **86/87** Cypress Gardens, AA/T Souter; **88/89** Bok Tower Gardens, AA/P Bennett; **90** Kissimmee Lake, AA/P Bennett; **91** Monument, AA/P Bennett; **92/93** Lake Tohopekaliga, Alamy/Rough Guides; **94** Wekiwa Springs, AA/P Bennett; **95** Wekiwa Spring State Park, AA/P Bennett; **96** Astronaut Hall of Fame, Kennedy Space Center, AA/T Souter; **96/97** Water Mania, Kissimmee, AA/P Bennett; **98** Golf Course, Winter Park, AA/P Bennett; **100** Heron, AA/P Bennett; **101** "Lights, Motor, Action!" Extreme Stunt Show, © Disney; **102** "Gertie" at Echo Lake, Disney-MGM Studios, © Disney; **104/105** Slush Gusher, Blizzard Beach, © Disney; **106/107** Animals carved in Tree of Life, © Disney; **108/109** Tree of Life Attraction, © Disney; **112/113** World of Disney store, © Disney; **114/115** Mission: SPACE, © Disney; **116** Spaceship Earth attraction at night, © Disney; **116/117** Japan Pavillion, © Disney; **118** Epcot® World Showcase, Aerial View, © Disney; **119** Italy Pavilion, © Disney; **120/121** Wishes Fireworks Show, © Disney; **122** The Jungle Cruise, © Disney; **122/123** Magic Carpets of Aladdin, © Disney; **124/125** Stitch's Great Escape, © Disney; **126/127** Fireworks at Downtown Disney Pleasure Island, © Disney; **128** Typhoon Lagoon Water Park, © Disney; **129** Classic Cars, Kissimmee, AA/P Bennett

Every effort has been made to trace the copyright holders, and we apologise in advance for any unintentional omissions or errors. We would be pleased to apply any corrections in any following edition of this publication.

Maps

Silver Springs

Orlando
★ Discovery Cove
★ SeaWorld
★ Wet 'n Wild
★ Universal Orlando®
  Resort
★ Harry P Leu Gardens

136-139 Orlando ★

140-143

Walt Disney
World® Resort ★

Kennedy
Space Center ★

Busch
Gardens ★

Cypress Gardens
Adventure Park ★

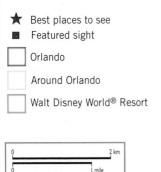

★ Best places to see
■ Featured sight
☐ Orlando
☐ Around Orlando
☐ Walt Disney World® Resort

0 ————————— 2 km
0 ————————— 1 mile

Cross Creek,
★ Silver Springs,
Wild Waters

Lake Griffin

Lake Yale

Umatilla Municiple Airport

COUNTY RD 452

Lake Eustis

LAKE YALE

COUNTY ROAD 44A

COUNTY RD 44

A

Bonaire Park

COUNTY RD 48

Lake Harris

STATE ROAD 44 E

COUNTY ROAD 46A

STATE HIGHWAY 46

1ST ST WEST

Central Florida
Zoological Park

Lake Mo

COUNTY ROAD 448

Little Lake Harris

COUNTY ROAD 561

PLYMOUTH

441

SORRENTO RD

B

COUNTY ROAD 33

FLORIDA'S TURNPIKE

COUNTY RD 455

VILLA CITY RD

STATE ROAD 19

Lake Apopka

OCOEE APOPKA RD

SILVER STAR RD

EDGEWATER DR

LEE RD

Winter
Park

ALOMA AVE

OVIE

C

STATE HIGHWAY 33

COUNTY ROAD 561

UNITED STATES HIGHWAY 27

COLONIAL DRIVE WEST

AVALON RD

AVALON ROAD

FLORIDA'S TURNPIKE

WINTER GARDEN VINELAND RD

TURKEY LAKE RD

KIRKMAN RD SOUTH

INTERNATIONAL DR

JOHN YOUNG PKY S

ORANGE BLOSSOM TRL S

EAST-WEST EXPRESSWAY

ORANGE AVE S

HOFFNER S

SEMORAN BLVD S

CURRY FO

BOGGY CREEK ROAD

Withlacoochee River

COUNTY ROAD 474

I-4

CENTRAL FLORIDA GREENEWAY

D

COMMONWEALTH AVE

COUNTY ROAD 557

COUNTY ROAD 655

VINE ST WEST

Green Meadows
Petting Farm

ORANGE BLOSSOM TRL S

COUNTY RD 54

Reedy Creek

HAM BROWN RD

PLEASANT HILL RD

Kissimmee

BOGGY CREEK ROAD

NEPTUNE RD

PARK RD

East Lak Tohopekal

Lake
Tohopekaliga

KISSIMMEE

Friars Cove

COX

Fantasy
of Flight

POLK CITY ROAD

I-4

KOA STREET

Cypress Lake

E

Busch
Gardens

COMBEE RD N

MEMORIAL BLVD E

WINTER LAKE RD

DUNDEE ROAD

Lake Marion

HATCHINEHA RD

Lake Hatchineha

Lake Pierce

F

Lake Hancock

COUNTY RD 540A EAST

Cypress Gardens
★ Adventure
Park

Lake Eloise

SCENIC HWY N

STATE ROAD 546

Historic Bok
Sanctuary

Lake
Wales

Lake Rosalie

Tiger Lake

Lake Kissim

STATE ROAD 60

80 FOOT RD

COX RD

STATE HIGHWAY 60

HESPERIDES ROAD

1   2   3   4

Lake Hancock
Lake Burden
OVERSTREET RD
FICQUETTE RD
GARDEN VINELAND ROAD
TIBET BUTLER DR

A

Lake Spar

Lake Huckleberry
LAKE HANCOCK RD
REAMS RD
Lake Reams
Lake Sharp
Lake Mabel

B

REAMS ROAD

Lake Lartigue
DUMP RD
FLORIDIAN WAY
CENTER DR
WORLD DR
Reedy Lake

Magic Kingdom®

Seven Seas Lagoon
Bay Lake

C

FLORIDIAN WAY
CENTER DR
WEST
WILDERNESS RD
Disney's Fort Wilderness
FORT WILDERNESS TRL
Osprey Ridge Golf Course
Magnolia Golf Course
SEVEN SEAS DR
BAY LAKE
FRONTIER WAY
Bannett Creek

WORLD DR
Eagle Pines Golf Course

D

Palm Golf Course
Whitenhouse Creek

★
WALT DISNEY WORLD® RESORT

VISTA BOUL
Bannett Creek
EPCOT CENTER

E

BEAR ISLAND ROAD
WORLD DRIVE
EPCOT RESORTS BOULEVARD
AVENUE OF THE STARS
Epcot®
World Showcase Lagoon

ORANGE LAKE BLVD E
ORANGE LAKE BLVD

Orange Lake Country Club & Resort
BUENA VISTA DRIVE
BUENA VISTA DRIVE

Disney's Animal Kingdom® Park
Blizzard Beach
Disney-MGM Studios

F

SPACE COAST PKWY
OSCEOLA PARKWAY WEST
OSCEOLA PARKWAY V

SHERBERTH RD
FORMOSA GDNS BLVD
Reedy Creek
Disney's Wide World of Sport

140

1   2   3   4

DOCTOR PHILLIPS

A
Lake Tibet
Lake Sheen
South Lake

B
Lake Sloat
Lake Tucker
Lake Serene
Big Sand Lake
Pocket Lake
Lake Crowell
Little Fish Lake
Grand Cypress Golf Resort

C
Little Sand Lake
Spring Lake
Sandy Lake

Ripley's Orlando Odditorium

SeaWorld

Discovery Cove

D
VINELAND
Lake Ruby
Lake Willis
Lake St
Vineland Ave
Lake Eve
Grande Pines Golf Course

E
Lake Buena Vista Golf Course
Village Lake
Pleasure Island
Downtown Disney
Typhoon Lagoon
Little Lake Bryan
Lake Bryan
World Center Golf Course

F
Falcons Fire Golf Course

WALLACE DRIVE
BAY HILL BOULEVARD
Golf Course
BAY DR S
GRANADA BLVD
CHAPELHILL DR
MARCELLA
SAND LAKE ROAD WEST
PONT CYPRESS DRIVE
KILGORE ROAD
APOPKA VINELAND ROAD SOUTH
DARLENE DRIVE
SANDSTONE DR
CHARLES ELIMPUS
BUENAVISTA WOODS BLVD
SMITH BENNETT RD
FENTON STREET
GRANBY ST
WINTER GARDEN-VINELAND ROAD
DOPEY DR
BONNET CREEK RD
COMMUNITY DR
CLUB LAKE DR
GRAND CYPRESS BLVD
HOTEL PLAZA BLVD
LAKE BUENA VISTA DRIVE
BUENA VISTA DRIVE
MEADOW DR
APOPKA VINELAND ROAD SOUTH
LANA DR
PALM PKY
LAKE ST
VINELAND AVE
LAKE WILLS DR
INTERNATIONAL DRIVE
HUNTER'S VISTA BLVD
WINTER GARDEN-VINELAND ROAD
WESTWOOD BOULEVARD
SEA HARBOR DRIVE
CENTRAL
TURKEY LAKE
I-4
INTERNATIONAL DRIVE
UNIVERSAL BOULEVARD
PERIMETER RD W
PERIMETER RD
UNIVERSAL
Wet 'n Wild

WINTER GARDEN-VINELAND ROAD

136
140
528
74A
72
71
68
67
65
6
417
3
536

INTERNATIONAL DRIVE
CENTRAL FLORIDA GREENEWAY
OSCEOLA
POLYNESIAN ISLES BLVD
PARKWAY WEST
VINELAND ROAD

142

A Communicarta **Style 45**® design

Cinderlane Parkway & Rosewood Way (302) (41) Apopka Superstop | Seminole Center (39)

Oxford Rd

North Lane

Denning Drive

Howel Branch Rd

(301)

Silver Star Road

Princetown St

Orange Ave

Aloma Ave & Forsyth Rd

Park Promenade Plaza

University Blvd

Goldenrod Rd & Bates Rd

West Oaks Mall (54)

John Young Parkway

(4) (7) (11) (21)
(29) (39) (54) (300)

Colonial Drive

(303)

Mills Ave

Semoran & Colonial

Hiawassee Rd

Ivy Lane

Lynx Central Station

Orlando Fashion Sq

Anderson St

Washington Shores

Gore Street

Poppy Ave

(304)

Kirkman Rd & Raleigh St

Orange Ave & Michigan St

Curry Ford Rd

Major Boulevard

Michigan St

Valencia Community College West

(301)

Holden Ave

Holden Ave

Kirkman Rd & Vineland Rd

Conroy Rd

Orange Ave & Oak Ridge Rd

Hansel Ave & Hoffner Ave

Gatlin Ave

Prime Outlets Orlando

Universal Parking Garage

Rio Grande Ave

Winegard Rd & Lancaster Rd

Wet 'n Wild

McCoy Rd & Daetwyler Dr

(21)

Florida Mall

Mandarin Drive & Sand Lake Road

(7)

Orange County Convention Center

Central Florida Pkwy

Orlando International Airport

SeaWorld

(11) (41) (42)

© Communicarta Ltd, 2008 UDN.3
Map user Ref: 9C02117/NPG/ORL/GB

Hunters Creek Blvd

Westwood Blvd & Central Florida Pkwy

Orlando Premium Outlets (42)

Principal timetabled calling points

Lynx Links

4	39
7	41
11	42
21	54
29	300-304

I-Ride Trolley Main Line
I-Ride Trolley Green Line

301 Disney's Animal Kingdom® Park & Epcot®
302 Magic Kingdom®
303 Disney-MGM Studios
304 Caribe Royal Resort

Vine St

(4) Kissimmee

144